Ergonomics- standards and guidelines for designers

Stephen Pheasant

Department of Anatomy,
Royal Free Hospital School of Medicine,
London

BSI
Linford Wood, Milton Keynes MK14 6LE
Telephone: 0908 221166

Published 1987 by British Standards Institution
BSI Catalogue number PP 7317:1987
UDC 65.015.11:685.512.2
ISBN 0 580 15391 6

Printed in Great Britain by
Richard Clay Ltd
Bungay, Suffolk NR35 1ED

Contents

List of illustrations

Page

List of tables

BSI Foreword

This book is for designers. They may be product designers, furniture designers, interior designers, or architects; they may be industrial designers, engineers, or teachers and students of design and technology—anybody who is designing a product or an area of activity for people.

The author has drawn his material from, in order of choice, international and British Standards, and the ergonomics literature in general. Standards are *not* quoted in their entirety and the author often expresses his own opinion.

Neither BSI nor the author can accept responsibility for any product or item made according to these guidelines. The designer is responsible for complying with legislation, and ensuring he or she is using complete, up-to-date information.

The sources for the book were the standards and documents which were in print in January 1987. Standards are continuously under review and revisions and amendments are published frequently. The status of standards may be checked by telephoning BSI's Enquiry Section on 0908 221166. The BSI Library at Milton Keynes holds a collection of over half a million international, British and foreign standards, laws, regulations and technical specifications.

Stewart Sanson
Head of Education, BSI

Part One
People

Section 1 Ergonomics and standards

If an object, an environment or a system is intended for human use, then its design should take into account the characteristics of its human users. We might call this way of looking at the design process 'user-centred'. Ergonomics is the science which deals with these matters. It may be defined as the application of scientific information concerning human beings to the problems of design. In the USA it is generally known as 'human factors'.

What do we mean when we assert that a particular product is 'ergonomically designed'? Sometimes, of course, the claim is just advertisers' hype. In order to justify it we require some kind of evidence that a satisfactory match between product and user has indeed been achieved. We might obtain such evidence by conducting a *user trial*—that is, an experiment in which a representative sample of people try out a mock up or prototype of the product, under carefully controlled conditions. The outcome might be evaluated in various ways. We should, of course, carefully record the opinions of the users as to factors such as comfort and functional simplicity. But, if it is possible, we should also endeavour to measure some objective index of performance or reliability. BS 6652 which deals with *Packagings resistant to opening by children* is essentially the specification for a user trial. It gives precise instructions as to how the subjects should be selected, how the experiment should be conducted, and how the results should be presented.

Is this the only way we can validate the claim that a product is ergonomically designed? Most ergonomists would consider that user trials are an essential part of every successful design project. But there is more to ergonomics than just *ad hoc* tests of usability. The resources of information, available in the literature of the subject, should enable us to predict, at the drawing board stage, whether or not a particular product will be acceptable to its human users. It may not always be possible to achieve this in practice, especially with new types of technology, but it is the direction in which the science of ergonomics should be heading. Most standards which deal directly with ergonomic issues take this latter approach. They specify good practice in the design of a particular type of product—as it is conceived on the basis of currently available evidence.

There is a sense in which any standardization of design is conducive to good ergonomic practice, in that it reduces the extent to which the user is presented with confusing information. Consider the problem of locating a house in an unfamiliar city street. You have every reason to suppose that the house numbers will be arranged sequentially on alternate sides of the road. You encounter an arrangement which does not conform to this hypothesis, become confused, waste energy walking up and down and curse the person who numbered the houses. Now it may well be that the alternate number/opposite side 'standard' is more logical or reasonable than any of the alternative arrangements which present themselves. But much more importantly, it is the arrangement which we have encountered most frequently in the past and therefore anticipate in the future. A relationship of this kind is known as a *stereotype* and many ergonomic recommendations fall into this category. ISO 4040, which deals with the controls of motor vehicles, is a good example. It does not matter much where you place the direction indicator (within reason). The important thing is that its location should be *consistent* in different vehicles, so that you don't operate the windscreen wipers each time you want to turn right.

Many people would argue (quite reasonably in my view) that everything that has been said so far is 'just common sense'. We all know that human beings are creatures of habit, bound by convention and easily confused by the unexpected. Does ergonomics have something more substantial to offer than a catalogue of expectations? The bulk of the substantive content of the discipline revolves around two key issues—human adaptability and human variability, both of which are measurable and both of which are amenable to standardization at least with respect to their limits.

Consider the physical environment at work. People can (and will) cope reasonably well with stuffy, noisy, poorly illuminated offices—but the process of adaptation may be a source of stress which has hidden costs in terms of frayed tempers, reduced working output, psychosomatic ill-health and a general reduction in the quality of life. Furthermore, there are limits to this adaptability, beyond which a more specific health risk may be deemed to exist. BS 5330, for example, deals with the relationship between the sound level to which people are exposed during an 8-hour working day and the predicted incidence of noise-induced hearing loss.

Human beings are highly variable—not least in the extent to which they are willing (or able) to tolerate bad design. Another aspect of their variability constitutes the subject matter of *anthropometrics*— the branch of ergonomics which deals with body size, shape and strength. Anthropometric data are particularly important in the design of furniture and workstations, where the relationships between the dimensions of the object and those of the user determine the latter's working posture and hence, to a great extent, his comfort and well being. (A good anthropometric match is necessary for comfort but not sufficient.)

BS 5940 Part 1 deals with the dimensions of office furniture. It includes a figure for (amongst other things) the range of adjustment in seat height which is deemed to be suitable for the majority of the working population. As an alternative, it also gives a single compromise value for a fixed height seat—which (we may

suppose) will minimize the overall degree of discomfort experienced in circumstances where an adjustable seat is inappropriate. (These considerations are not made explicit in the standard—but most ergonomists would probably see things in these terms.) As a general rule, ergonomics seeks to achieve the greatest possible level of comfort (or other satisfaction) for the greatest possible number of users—within the limits set by whatever constraints circumstances might impose. In some cases it may be appropriate to base our design, not upon the capacities and limitations of the broad majority, but upon those of a minority of users who are disadvantaged in some way. BS 5619 and BS 5810 deal with the requirements of disabled people—particularly wheelchair users and those with hearing or sight impairments.

Some general principles, concerning the applications of ergonomics in the design of work systems, are presented in outline in ISO 6385. It deals with the design of furniture and other equipment in the work space; with physical environmental factors; and with the design of the work process and the avoidance of underloading or overloading the working person. It does not give detailed specifications concerning these matters—but it lists the factors which should be taken into account. (The standard is reproduced in full in appendix A, with cross-references to sections in this book.)

In this book, we shall draw on existing British and international standards wherever possible. But there are areas of ergonomic thinking which are not yet incorporated into standards, (either because they deal with new technologies or because research is not yet sufficiently advanced). Perhaps the most important ergonomic issues of the present moment concern our propensity for creating products, environments and systems which are beyond the comprehension of their users. In these cases I shall attempt to summarize such tentative guidelines as are presently available. These have been compiled from a wide range of sources, some of which are more comprehensive or better established than others. I hope that the selection which is presented is a reasonably accurate reflection of the current 'state of the art' in ergonomics.

It must be acknowledged, however, that many ergonomists have severe misgivings about design recommendations of this kind. They would argue that, since each design problem is unique, all standards and guidelines are necessarily an oversimplification of a complex set of issues which are best studied empirically. Such a viewpoint would seem to condemn us to an endless process of re-inventing the wheel. But it is true that the recommendations of this (or any other) ergonomics book should be used with discretion. Ultimately it is up to the designer to decide whether a particular recommendation is relevant to his or her particular problem—and when in doubt to initiate an empirical investigation of the issues involved.

Section 2 Principles of anthropometrics

Anthropometrics is the branch of ergonomics which deals with body measurements, particularly those of size, strength and physical capacity.

2.1 The statistical distribution of anthropometric data

In most ergonomic applications, it is necessary to make provision for the range of variability, in a particular characteristic, which we expect to encounter in our user population. This variability may generally be described by a mathematical function, called the *normal distribution*, which has the form of a bell-shaped curve (see figure 2.1). Plotted horizontally is the magnitude of the dimension concerned. Plotted vertically is the frequency with which we would expect to encounter a person of that particular size, (or the probability of encountering such a person).

The curve is symmetrical about the average (or mean) value which is also the point of maximum probability. Since 50% of the population is smaller than the average value, it is also known as the 50th percentile (50%le). Equidistant on either side of this point, are two values which bracket the middle 90% of the population. The lower of these values is known as the 5th percentile and the upper is known as the 95th percentile. In general *n*% of the population is smaller than the *n*th percentile.

A minority of anthropometric measurements (particularly body girths) is not symmetrically distributed about the mean—in these cases the 5th percentile is closer to the 50th than the 95th. (Hence, there are more fat people than the symmetrical normal distribution would predict—and fewer thin ones.) Such a distribution is said to be *positively skewed*.

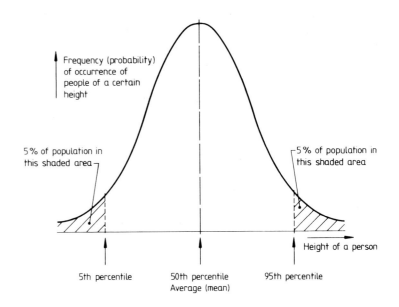

Figure 2.1 The normal distribution

2.2 Choosing the most appropriate percentile

In specifying the dimensions of furniture, workstations, etc., it is considered good practice to design for those members of the user population who fall between the 5th and 95th percentiles in any particular respect. Hence, 90% (or in some cases 95%) of users is *accommodated* within the *design limits*. In cases where we are required to provide *clearance* for the user, the 95th percentile value of the relevant dimension should be employed—hence, the 95% of users who are smaller than this will necessarily be accommodated. By the same token, in dealing with matters of *reach* we should use 5th percentile values—hence accommodating the 95% of the population who can reach further. There are other cases, such as the heights of seats and working surfaces, where neither the tall nor the short person is self-evidently more worthy of consideration. In these cases an adjustable workstation is commonly the best solution, and we would choose a range of adjustment to match the 5th to 95th percentiles (hence accommodating 90 % of users). Where an adjustable device is not appropriate (by reason of cost or complexity) it may be possible to settle for a single compromise value which will minimize the overall level of inconvenience or discomfort suffered. (This is not always a simple matter.)

By definition, a workstation designed for the 5th to 95th percentile range of users will mis-match (or fail to accommodate) the remaining 10 % who are outside the design limits. (Furthermore, in a complex workstation design problem, where several different body dimensions act as constraints, we might expect a different 10 % to be excluded each time.) Does this matter? Usually not, since people are adaptable and the criteria which define an effective match are usually fuzzy rather than sharp.

In critical applications, where a mis-match might have severe consequences, it may be necessary to apply wider design limits such as the 1st and 99th percentiles. These have not been tabulated, but they may be easily calculated. First it is necessary to find a parameter of the relevant normal distribution, called the *standard deviation (s)*, given by the equation

$$s = (95\%\text{le}-5\%\text{le})/3.28.$$

The 1st and 99th percentiles are then given by

$$50\%\text{le} \pm 2.33s$$

In exceptional cases, such as the calculation of safety clearances, design limits of $50\%\text{le} \pm 3s$ may be appropriate.

Figure 2.1 shows that extremely large or small people are increasingly infrequent, the further they depart from the average (50 %le). In essence, this means that the accommodation of these extremes is likely to be increasingly expensive—particularly when it comes to adjustable equipment or products in a range of sizes. Deciding where to stop is a matter of judgement in each individual case.

Additional information-For a general discussion of the principles and practice of anthropometrics see PP 7310 and Pheasant (1986).

Section 3 Static anthropometric data

The data given in this section are all examples of *static* measurements made on unclothed subjects, in standardized postures (as shown in the accompanying diagrams). Where these conditions do not apply, it is necessary to make *ad hoc* corrections, examples of which are given below.

The anthropometric characteristics of any given population are dependent upon such factors as sex, age, ethnicity, social class/occupation and nutritional status. Anthropometric surveys, on a scale large enough to give reliable results, are costly, time consuming and extremely tedious. Consequently, there is a dearth of reliable information for all except a few specialized user populations (most of whom are in the armed forces).

The figures given in table 3.1 are best estimates, in the light of currently available evidence, of the body dimensions of the general population of Great Britain aged 19 to 65 years. Most of the data were calculated by approximate statistical methods, as described in Pheasant (1986), from which they are quoted. Other sources consulted included Knight (1984), WIRA (1980) and Kemsley (1957). The data are a revised (and, it is hoped, improved) version of the figures given in PP 7310; and they must necessarily serve, until such time as a definitive survey of the population of Great Britain has been conducted. (It seems unlikely that such a survey will be undertaken in the foreseeable future.)

3.1 Clothing corrections

The data given here refer to unclothed, unshod people. It will commonly be necessary, therefore, to add corrections for whatever shoes and clothing users are likely to be wearing. These are a matter for common sense and discretion. The following examples should serve as a general guide:

- For the heels of shoes, worn outdoors or in semi-formal situations, add 25 mm for men or 45 mm for women, to all standing or sitting dimensions measured from ground level. For ordinary street shoes add 30 mm to the length of the foot.
- For industrial safety helmets, add 35 mm to standing and sitting height.
- For heavy outdoor clothing add 40 mm to shoulder breadth and other dimensions concerned with clearance and access.

In general, no corrections are required for ordinary indoor clothing (other than for shoes, as given above).

Additional information—See PP 7310 and Pheasant (1986). The latter contains anthropometric estimates for the British population of all ages (from the new born to the elderly) and adult data for various other nationalities.

Table 3.1 Anthropometric estimates for British adults (19–65 years)

Dimensions in mm. Percentiles rounded to nearest 5 mm, as appropriate.

	Men			Women		
	5th %le	50th %le	95th %le	5th %le	50th %le	95th %le
Body weight (kg)	55	75	94	44	63	81
1 Stature	1625	1740	1855	1505	1610	1710
2 Eye height	1515	1630	1745	1405	1505	1610
3 Neck height	1375	1485	1595	1280	1375	1470
4 Shoulder height	1315	1425	1535	1215	1310	1405
5 Chest (bust) height	1175	1270	1365	1080	1170	1255
6 Elbow height	1005	1090	1180	930	1005	1085
7 Hip height	840	920	1000	740	810	885
8 Knuckle height	690	755	820	660	720	780
9 Fingertip height	590	655	720	560	625	685
10 Sitting height	850	910	965	795	850	910
11 Sitting eye height	730	790	845	685	740	795
12 Sitting shoulder height	540	595	645	505	555	610
13 Sitting elbow height	190	245	295	185	235	280
14 Thigh thickness	135	160	185	125	155	180
15 Buttock–knee length	545	595	645	520	570	620
16 Buttock–popliteal length	440	495	550	435	480	530
17 Knee height	495	545	595	455	500	540
18 Popliteal height	395	440	490	355	400	445
19 Shoulder breadth (bideltoid)	420	465	510	355	395	435
20 Shoulder breadth (biacromial)	365	400	430	325	355	385
21 Elbow–elbow breadth	390	450	510	300	385	475
22 Hip breadth	310	360	405	310	370	435
23 Chest (bust) depth	215	250	285	210	250	295
24 Abdominal depth	220	270	320	205	255	305

Notes

Dimensions 10 to 12 These measurements are made in an erect sitting position; in reality people tend to slump. To allow for this subtract 40 mm (if appropriate).

Dimensions 16 and 18 The popliteal region is the back of the knee.

Dimension 19 Measured across the shoulders at the broadest points (i.e. the deltoid muscles).

Dimension 20 Measured between the bony tips of the shoulder (known to anatomists as the acromion processes).

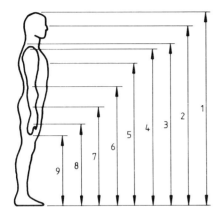

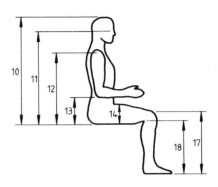

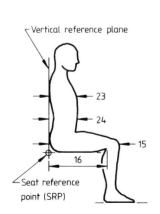

Vertical reference plane

Seat reference point (SRP)

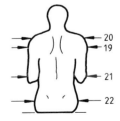

Table 3.1 (continued)

	Men			Women		
	5th %le	50th %le	95th %le	5th %le	50th %le	95th %le
25 Shoulder-fingertip length	720	780	840	655	705	760
26 Shoulder-elbow length	330	365	395	300	330	360
27 Elbow-fingertip length	440	475	510	400	430	460
28 Span	1655	1790	1925	1490	1605	1725
29 Elbow span	865	945	1020	780	850	920
30 Vertical reach	2040	2170	2300	1895	2010	2125
31 Sitting vertical reach	1255	1355	1455	1150	1255	1340
32 Horizontal reach	835	890	945	760	810	860
33 Hand length	173	189	205	159	174	189
34 Hand breadth (metacarpal)	78	87	95	69	76	83
35 Hand breadth (including thumb)	97	105	114	84	92	99
36 Hand girth	201	216	236	169	184	199
37 Palm length	98	107	116	89	97	105
38 Index finger length	64	72	79	60	67	74
39 Index finger breadth	19	21	24	16	18	20
40 Hand thickness at palm	27	33	38	24	28	33
41 Hand thickness (including thumb)	44	51	58	40	45	50
42 Maximum grip diameter	45	52	59	43	48	53
43 Foot length	240	265	285	215	235	255
44 Foot breadth	85	95	110	80	90	100
45 Foot girth	220	245	270	210	225	245
46 Heel-ball length	175	190	210	160	175	190
47 Ankle height	60	70	85	55	65	75

Notes

Dimensions 30 to 32 These are fingertip measures:

- For a full grasping action subtract 60% of hand length (or 110 mm).

- For actions involving a pinchgrip (as in operating a rotary knob, etc.) subtract 40% of hand length (or 75 mm).

The figures given are all 'easy' reaches made with minimal movements of the trunk or the shoulder girdle. Hence in the case of forward horizontal reach (dimension 32), if the shoulder blades were touching a wall at the outset, they would still be doing so when the measurement was taken. For a forward thrusting action of the shoulder add 100 mm to dimension 32; and for a 20° forward inclination of the trunk add a further 150 mm.

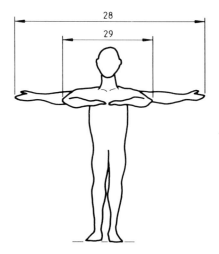

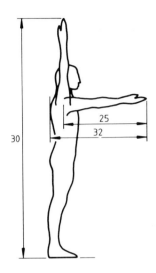

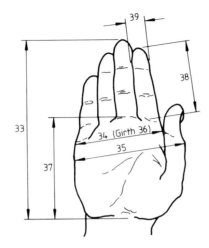

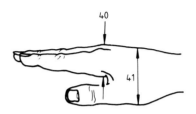

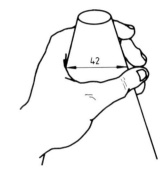

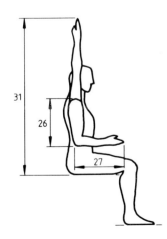

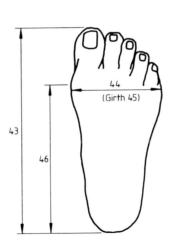

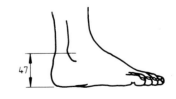

Table 3.1 (concluded)

	Men			Women		
	5th %le	50th %le	95th %le	5th %le	50th %le	95th %le
48 Head length	180	195	205	165	180	190
49 Head breadth	145	155	165	135	145	155
50 Head height	205	225	240	200	220	240
51 Head girth	535	565	590	525	550	575
52 Ear-ear breadth	125	135	145	120	130	135
53 Inter-pupillary breadth	55	60	70	55	60	65
54 Maximum diameter from chin	240	255	265	225	235	245
55 Nose-back of head	205	220	235	190	205	220
56 Coronal arc	330	350	375	315	340	360
57 Sagittal arc	350	380	405	325	350	375
58 Neck girth	345	375	425	335	365	415
59 Chest (bust) girth	840	950	1110	820	935	1135
60 Underbust girth	—	—	—	675	775	940
61 Waist girth	705	805	965	565	685	885
62 Hip girth	890	965	1060	885	985	1165
63 Waist height	905	1075	1150	920	1005	1085
64 Crotch height	760	840	920	675	750	825
65 Waist front	360	410	460	305	355	405
66 Waist back	390	450	510	365	405	445
67 Interscye	320	375	425	305	350	395
68 Sleeve length (spine–wrist)	810	875	940	735	790	835
69 Maximum body breadth	480	530	580	355	420	485
70 Maximum body depth	255	290	325	225	275	325
71 Kneeling height	1210	1295	1380	1130	1205	1280
72 Buttock-heel length	985	1070	1160	875	965	1055

Notes

Dimension 56 Measured from ear to ear over the top of the head.

Dimension 57 Measured from the brow to the back of the head (occiput) over the top of the head.

Dimensions 63 and 64 are approximately equal to the tailoring measures 'outside leg' and 'inside leg' respectively.

Dimensions 69 and 70 are overall measures, taken at the broadest and deepest points wherever they may be.

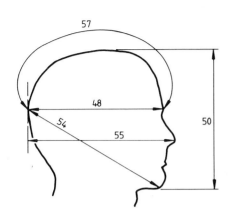

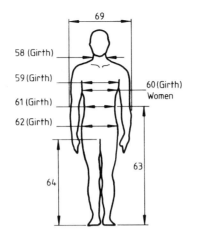

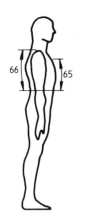

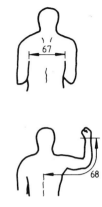

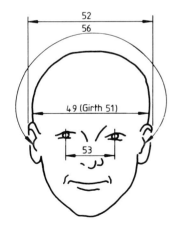

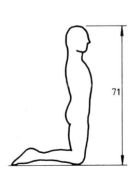

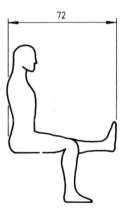

Section 4 Access and clearance

Many of the data in table 3.1 are applicable to problems of access and clearance (the 95th percentile male value will usually be the most relevant). This section deals with some special cases.

4.1 Handles and hand grips

Minimum acceptable clearance dimensions for hand grips and handles are given in table 4.1.

Table 4.2 shows the minimum diameter D of curvature of the edge of the handle as a function of the loading to which it will be exposed (e.g. the weight of an item to be carried). Gripping efficiency is best if the hand can wrap around to an angle of 120° or more (see also sections 7.3, 7.4 and 20.3).

4.2 Manual access

Maintenance tasks (for example) commonly involve *reaching into* a piece of equipment. The apertures given in table 4.3 are just large enough to admit the 95th percentile male finger, hand or arm (as the case may be). The table is based partly on ISO 2860, which deals with earth moving machinery, and partly on MIL-STD-1472C. Since the latter is intended for US military personnel, who are larger in most respects than most other populations, it should be generally applicable. Where both sources give a value for the same dimension, the larger has been quoted. The data in table 4.3 are for bare handed, lightly clad persons. (The original sources also give data for gloved and heavily clad persons.)

These apertures will not, in general, give visual access.

Table 4.1 Minimum dimensions of handles

Dimensions in mm.

Type of grip	Bare hand			Gloved hand		
	Dimension			Dimension		
	X	Y	Z	X	Y	Z
Two fingers	32	65	75	38	75	75
One hand	48	111	75	50	125	100
Two hands	48	215	75	50	270	100

From MIL-STD-1472C

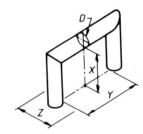

Table 4.2 Minimum curvature of handle or edge

Dimensions in mm.

Load	Minimum diameter D
Up to 65 N	6
65 N to 90 N	13
90 N to 175 N	19
over 175 N	25

From MIL-STD-1472C. The loadings have been converted to newtons and rounded to the nearest 5.

Table 4.3 Minimum acceptable aperture dimensions for manual access

Dimensions in mm

| | Note | Rectangular opening | | Circular opening |
		Length L	Width or height W	Diameter D
Fingertip to first joint				
Push button	a	—	—	32
Two-finger twisting action	a			object + 50
Empty hand to wrist	b	110	65	110
Clenched hand to wrist	a	125	95	125
Hand plus 25 diameter object (e.g. screwdriver)	a	95	95	95
Hand plus object larger than 25	a	45 clearance around object		
One arm to shoulder	b	200	150	200
Inserting box with two hands	c	width of box + 115	—	—
Reaching with both hands to a depth R	b	$3/4R$ + width of object + 115 (min. 200; max. 560)	150	—

Notes to table 4.3:

1 Sources:
  a MIL-STD-1472C quoted, no value given in ISO 2860;
  b ISO 2860 quoted, MIL-STD 1472C gives a smaller value;
  c both sources give the same value.

2 MIL-STD-1472C quotes limiting values for the dimension R of 150 mm and 490 mm. The latter figure is based on a study of the reaching capacity of male military personnel, described in van Cott and Kinkade (1972). The two-handed functional reach into an aperture is approximately 450 mm for a 5th percentile woman.

4.3 Whole body access

Occasionally it is necessary for a person to climb through a hatch or some similar opening. Minimum dimensions are given in table 4.4.

Table 4.4 Whole body access

Minimum dimension in mm	Square	Round	Rectangular	
	$W = L$	D	W	L
Normal clothing	520	560	330	560
Arctic clothing	600	650	470	650

Note.   Maximum 25 radius optional on all corners

From ISO 2860

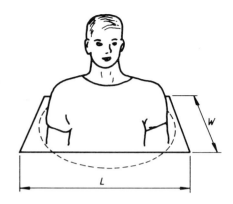

Comment—ISO 2860 states that 'the recommended openings are the smallest that will accommodate 95 % of the worldwide operator population'. By inference, this means that 5 % of operators will get stuck, which may well be acceptable since the standard deals with 'openings provided . . . for purposes of inspection, adjustment and maintenance'. The data of table 3.1 confirm that a 95th percentile man could pass through with just a little leeway. For emergency purposes a larger opening would be required.

Additional information—Circulation and access in buildings is the subject of section 20.

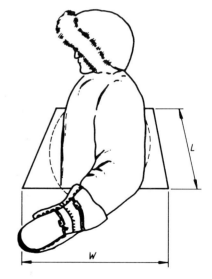

Section 5 Reach envelopes

The data of table 3.1 may be used to define the zone of convenient reach—i.e. the volume of space which is 'within arm's length'. The upper limit of this zone is given by *vertical reach* (standing dimension 30 or sitting dimension 31); its lower limit in the standing position by *fingertip height* (dimension 9); its forward extent by *horizontal reach* (dimension 32); and its lateral extent by *span* (dimension 28). We would generally use 5th percentile values (except for fingertip height where the 95th percentile may well be more appropriate). The remainder of the zone, viewed in elevation or plan, can be sketched in quite easily (see figure 5.1).

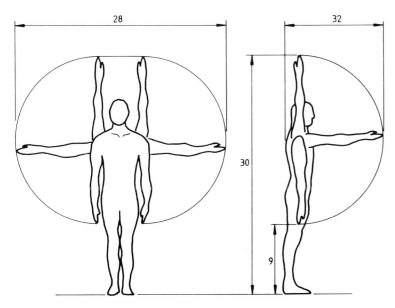

Figure 5.1 Zone of convenient reach

The above data are all *static* measures—they were made with minimal effort, without bending, twisting etc. Sometimes, in complicated workstations, it is not possible to keep everything within arm's length. In such cases, *dynamic* data are required—describing the maximum rather than the convenient reach. The dynamic reach envelope (as the space thus defined is called) is primarily important in the design of sitting workstations—since the standing operator is generally less fixed to a single position. The distance you can reach in a sitting position depends (among other things) upon the design of the seat itself and whether or not you are wearing any kind of restraint (such as a seat belt). It is not possible, therefore, to provide dynamic reach data which are generally applicable to all circumstances.

The data given in tables 5.1a and 5.1b deal with the location of controls in road vehicles (cars, trucks, etc.). ISO 3958 defines the seat configuration in any particular vehicle by means of a 'package factor', which is based on certain measurements of the driver's workstation, the exact details of which need not concern us here.

Table 5.1a is for a 'package factor' which is equivalent to that of a typical family saloon car; 5.1b is for a heavy truck. The reaches in the latter case are greater—presumably because the seat is more upright. ISO 3958 provides data for user populations made up of men and women in various proportions. The data given here are 5th percentile values for a user population in which men and women are equally represented.

Notes to tables are on page 20.

Table 5.1a Hand-reach envelope — family car

Dimensions in mm

Elevation above H-point	Stations outboard of centre line							Stations inboard of centre line								
	400	300	250	200	100	50	0	0	50	100	200	250	300	400	500	600
800	394	445	464	478	498	505	511	507	516	519	510	498	483	443	395	
700	469	512	527	538	553	559	564	562	576	580	571	561	548	515	472	
600	524	560	573	583	593	594	593	601	617	623	618	610	599	570	529	463
500	560	591	603	612	616	610	598	623	639	648	650	644	636	609	566	498
450	571	600	612	621	622	612	593	628	643	654	660	657	649	622	576	510
400	578	604	617	626	624					655	667	666	659	631	582	517
350	580	604	618	627	623					652	670	671	666	636	583	520
300	578	601	615	626	618					644	669	673	669	636	579	519
250	571	593	608	620	609					632	665	672	669	633	569	514
200	561	581	598	611	597					615	657	667	665	626	555	505
100	527	545	566	583							630	647	648	599	512	474
0	478	494	521	542							588	614	618	556	450	
−100	412	429	461	487							532	567	574	497	368	

From ISO 3958

Table 5.1b Hand-reach envelope — heavy truck

Dimensions in mm

Elevation above H-point	Stations outboard of centre line							Stations inboard of centre line								
	400	300	250	200	100	50	0	0	50	100	200	250	300	400	500	600
800	408	460	479	494	515	522	528	534	547	551	541	529	514	477	430	
700	480	525	540	552	568	574	579	587	603	609	601	591	579	548	505	
600	533	571	585	595	606	608	608	622	639	647	645	638	629	601	558	590
500	568	600	613	622	629	625	615	640	656	667	674	671	664	636	590	523
450	579	608	621	630	635	627	611	643	658	670	683	682	676	647	598	533
400	586	612	625	635	637					668	687	689	684	654	601	538
350	588	612	625	636	636					662	689	693	690	657	599	540
300	586	607	622	633						652	686	694	691	655	592	537
250	580	598	614	627						638	680	691	690	650	580	530
200	569	585	603	617						619	671	685	685	641	564	520
100	535	547	568	587							641	663	665	611	517	486
0	485	493	519	542							598	628	633	566	453	438
−100	418	423	455	484							541	580	588	506	371	374

From ISO 3958

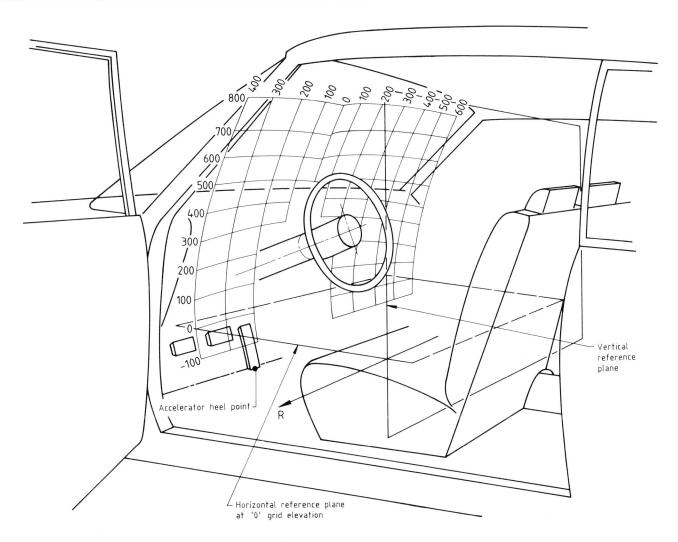

Figure 5.2 Hand–reach envelope of person in driving seat   From ISO 3958

Notes to tables 5.1a and 5.1b (not part of ISO 3958):

1   The figures tabulated are forward reaches measured from a vertical reference plane, at various distances above a horizontal reference plane. These intersect along the line R (in figure 5.2) which represents the location of the operator's hip joint (i.e. the pivot point at which his trunk and lower limbs articulate). The exact definition of R is complicated. For most purposes it is equivalent to another reference index known as the H-point. Strictly speaking they should be determined, for a particular seat, by using a special two dimensional template (for R) or three dimensional dummy (for H) as described in ISO 6549. Most designers outside the automotive industry work from the *seat reference point* (SRP) which is defined by the intersection of the plane which best approximates the compressed seat surface, the plane which best approximates the compressed backrest, and the median (mid-line) plane of the body. To convert from one system to the other we may assume that:
— the H (R) point is 97 mm above the plane of the compressed seat surface;
— the H (R) point is 135 mm in front of the plane of the compressed seat back.
A number of variations on the theme of the H–point or the SRP are to be found in the literature. Space and the finite duration of human patience (both mine and yours) prevent us from discussing them here.

2   The reaches tabulated are for a pinch-grip reach, using three fingers (as in operating a 25 mm control knob). For fingertip operation add 40 % hand length (or 75 mm); for full hand grasp subtract 20 % hand length (or 40 mm).

3   ISO 3958 is based on a survey of a representative sample of drivers in the USA. The figures may therefore slightly over-estimate the reaches of European populations—a deduction of 10 mm from all tabulated values should be enough to account for this difference. The subjects in the original experiment wore a non-extensible seat belt—hence the shorter reaches for positions inboard of the centre line (i.e. to the right in a left-hand drive car). For applications in which seat belts are not worn it should be assumed that the reach values for outboard positions will be symmetrically repeated either side of the mid-line.

Section 6 Biomechanics

The most appropriate posture for the performance of any particular task is the one which allows it to be accomplished with the least muscular effort. Strength is the capacity to exert force in the execution of a particular task. If the limbs or trunk are used in a position of poor mechanical advantage, their capacity to exert force will be diminished. The differences in strength, which thus result from differences in posture, may be as great (or greater) than those which result from variation in muscular endowment. The science which deals with these matters is called *biomechanics*.

The over-use (or mis-use) of the muscles, joints and asssociated soft tissues, may lead to a variety of painful and disabling conditions. Back pain, neck pain, shoulder pain and repetitive strain injuries of the wrist and forearm are of particular interest in the context of ergonomics—since they are commonly attributable to faulty workspace design or excessive task demands. Within reasonable limits dynamic muscular activity, involving both contraction and relaxation (stretching), is probably beneficial rather than otherwise; but excessive repetitions of a particular movement (especially if these are rapid and vigorous) may well be harmful. Muscle strains (and the tissue inflammation which results) are rarely caused by a single excessive effort—more commonly, the damage is cumulative.

Prolonged muscle efforts, in a fixed position, lead rapidly to fatigue and should be avoided wherever possible. *Static muscle exertion is generally postural – it results from the need to support the weight of the limbs or trunk against the force of gravity.* How is this to be avoided? The following should serve as a general guide.

6.1 Guidelines concerning working posture

Wherever possible avoid fixed working postures; allow operator to alternate between standing and sitting, etc.

- *Controls* or *working surfaces* which are *too low* cause the user to stoop (i.e. to incline his trunk forward); this imposes a static load on the back muscles (which support the weight of the trunk).

- *Controls* or *working surfaces* which are *too high* will cause the user to adopt unsatisfactory postures of the upper limb (and load the shoulder muscles).

- *The optimum height of a working surface* for a standing user depends upon the task to be performed. The following working heights are recommended:
  — For manipulative tasks involving moderate degrees of both force and precision a working level between 50 mm and 100 mm below elbow height. (For the general population of adult men and women this either means a worktop adjustable between 900 mm and 1100 mm or a compromise value of 1000 mm.)
  — For delicate tasks, 50 mm to 100 mm above elbow height (wrist supports are often desirable).
  — For heavy tasks (especially involving downward pressure on the workpiece) a lower level (e.g. 100 mm to 300 mm below elbow height).
  — Note that in calculating working height it is necessary to allow for the size of objects which will be used on the working surface.

- *Visual displays* which are *too low* cause the user to incline his head, which imposes a strain on the neck muscles. In conventional office work and certain industrial assembly tasks the focus of visual attention is on the table surface. Sloping desks and raised reading stands may well be advantageous. (Location of displays is discussed in section 14.2.)

- In order to avoid *twisted and asymmetric* postures, frequently used displays and controls should be located directly in front of the body.

- In general, the most comfortable postures are those which employ the middle third of the range of motions of any particular joint.

- In the *sitting position*, the weight of the trunk should be supported, as far as is practicable, by the backrest of the seat. This should incline backwards from the vertical by as much as 20° and be of adequate height to support the shoulders (600 mm) or preferably the back of the head (850 mm). If a reclined position is not compatible with the visual or manual demands of the task (as in reading and writing) then an upright position is next best. The *backrest* should also help maintain the natural curve of the spine—it should therefore be slightly convex in the lumbar region—at around 230 mm above the seat surface if fixed, or from 170 mm to 300 mm if adjustable. (Seat design is discussed in section 22.)

- *Lifting and handling tasks* performed in a stooped position (with the trunk inclined forward or to the sides) are particularly hazardous. The strength and stability of the lifting action is greatest when the effective axis of the lift is kept as close as possible to the body. In practice this is dependent on foot placement and the bulk of the load. Avoid reaching over or into things. Lifting strength is greatest at around knuckle height (700 mm to 800 mm).

- Two-handed *pushing or pulling actions* (in the standing position) are best performed at a little below elbow height (around 1100 mm for men and 1000 mm for women). Pushing actions are strongest when the feet are placed as far back as possible (or when the body is braced against a firm support). Pulling actions are strongest when the feet are placed as far forward as possible (avoid obstacles for the feet). High-friction shoes and flooring materials are essential; an unobstructed floor space of 1000 mm is required (1800 mm is preferable for pushing tasks).

- The strength of either a thrusting or a pulling action will be greatest when the line of force approximates to that of a straight (or almost straight) limb (see section 7.5).

Additional information—Grandjean (1981), Singleton (1982, Ch 3), and Pheasant (1986).

Section 7 Strength

The force which a person is able to exert, in the performance of a particular task, is dependent on numerous factors. Some of these concern the person, others concern the task. The relationship between strength and posture has already been discussed.

7.1 Sex and age

In general, the strength of the average woman is around 60% of that of the average man. Both men and women are greatest in strength at around 30 years of age; they have reached 90% of this maximum by 20; they decline to 90% by 45 and to 75–80% by 60. However, there is considerable variation *between tasks* in the magnitude of the sex difference (Pheasant 1983) and some variation in the magnitude of the age differences. It is not therefore possible to generalize with any degree of accuracy. Furthermore, the differences within each sex or age group (owing to physique, training, etc.) are greater than those between sexes or age groups. Hence, there is considerable overlap between the strongest woman and the weakest man and between the strongest 60 year old and the weakest 30 year old.

7.2 Duration and repetition

Maximum strength can be exerted for a few seconds only. A steady force of approximately half maximum can be sustained for one minute and 15% maximum can be exerted more or less indefinitely. (Note that this applies to continuous exertions; intermittent efforts can be sustained much longer.)

What percentage of a person's maximum strength can we expect him (or her) to exert in the execution of a particular task? Most ergonomists would probably accept the following rules of thumb:

- Exertions of greater than 60% maximum are to be avoided if at all possible;
- For occasional efforts, up to 60% maximum is acceptable;
- For frequent actions, up to 30% maximum is acceptable;
- For continuous actions, up to 15% maximum is acceptable, but these should be avoided wherever possible.

Note—When tabulating design data it is not always possible to take into account the numerous factors which influence human strength. The figures which follow are intended as a general guide only. They are best thought of as order-of-magnitude estimates.

7.3 Grip strength

Table 7.1 Grip strengths

5th %le male in newtons	Momentary hold	Sustained hold
Full grip		
— Left hand	250	145
— Right hand	260	155
Pinch grip	60	35

From MIL-STD-1472C

Table 7.1 gives 5th percentile male grip strengths. The full grip is a squeezing action using the fingers and the palm of the hand; the pinch grip uses the thumb and index finger. The data are (presumably) based on military personnel—but comparison with other sources suggests that they will be reasonably representative of young men in general. The standard suggests that two-thirds of the tabulated value would be reasonable for women—but evidence in the literature (Pheasant 1983) suggests that this might over-estimate the strength of the 5th percentile woman and that half the quoted values would be safer.

Comments—The 'momentary hold' values represent the maximal exertion of a weak member of the population; sustained holds were (presumably) calculated on the basis of the strength/endurance relationship given above. The source of the data is not given in the standard, but comparison with other published material suggests that the figures are reasonably representative of young adult men and women.

The strength of a gripping action is dependent upon the size of the object which is gripped. For pivoting tools, such as pliers, a handle separation of 45 mm to 55 mm is optimal for both men and women. (The 'full grip' data given above are for an optimally sized handle of this type.) For cylindrical handles a diameter of 30 mm to 50 mm is optimal for thrusts along the axis of the handle and 50 mm to 65 mm for twists about the axis of the handle (Pheasant 1986). Note that a cylindrical handle, gripped in the palm of the hand, will make an angle of around 110° with the axis of the forearm (when the wrist is in its comfortable neutral position).

7.4 Finger strength

The data given in table 7.2 are 5th percentile values, based on a study of US men which is quoted in both Damon et al. (1966) and in van Cott and Kinkade (1972). Measurements were made of the force which could be exerted using the tip of an extended (straight) finger. Women might reasonably be expected to exert 50 % of these forces.

Table 7.2 Finger strengths

5th %ile male values in newtons, rounded to nearest 5

	Strength
Thumb	45
Index finger	35
Middle finger	30
Ring finger	20
Little finger	15

In a pulling action using one hooked finger, or a poking action using one straight finger the 5th percentile man could be expected to exert 35 N and the 5th percentile woman about half of this (Woodson 1981).

7.5 Arm strength

Data for maximal efforts in one-handed pushing and pulling actions in the sitting position are given in table 7.3. These are 5th percentile values for US military personnel. The standard recommends a reduction to two-thirds of the quoted value for women. This may over estimate the strength of a 5th percentile woman— half the quoted values would be safer.

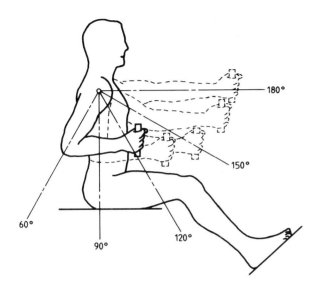

Table 7.4 Percentage reductions in the acceptable forces shown in figures 7.1 to 7.3 according to frequency of exertion

Population	Frequency of exertion	
	Less than one per minute	More than one per minute
Men under 50	—	30
Women under 50	40	45
Men over 50	20	58
Women over 50	52	66

Table 7.3 Arm strengths

Forces in newtons, rounded to nearest 5

Elbow angle (deg)	Push		Pull	
	Right	Left	Right	Left
180	220	185	230	220
150	185	135	250	185
120	160	115	185	150
90	160	100	165	140
60	150	100	105	115

From MIL-STD-1472 C

7.6 Whole body activities

The data of figures 7.1 to 7.3, which are extracts from an extensive collection in DEF STAN 00-25 (Part 3)/1, are not strength measurements in the conventional sense. They are estimates of the forces which 95 % of the members of a given population can be reasonably expected to exert, under given conditions, without risk of injury (either immediate or cumulative). The criteria on which the recommendations are based are discussed in Davis and Stubbs (1977, 1978).

The values shown in the diagrams represent the capacity of a 5th percentile adult man, under 50 years of age, working at a rate of less than one exertion per minute. For other conditions, the load should be *reduced* by the amounts shown in table 7.4. Note that in each case the loads are given in newtons which have been converted from the kgf of the original source and, in the process of doing so, have been rounded *down* to the nearest five. The centre of each contour chart is the acromion—that is, the bony tip of the shoulder.

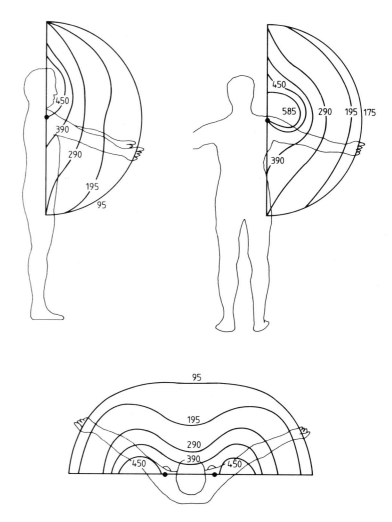

Figure 7.1 Acceptable two-handed lifting forces in standing position
From DEF STAN 00-25 (Part 3)/1

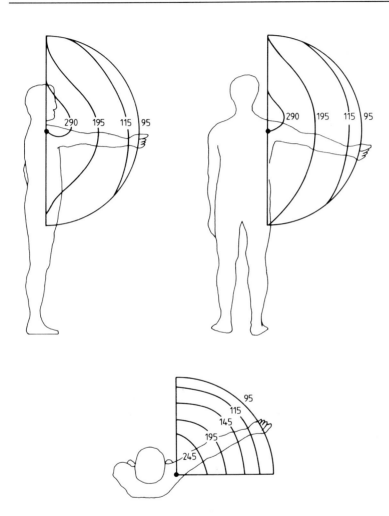

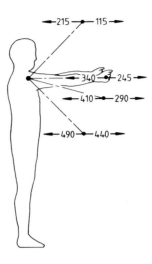

Figure 7.3 Acceptable two-handing pushing and pulling forces in the standing position   From DEF STAN 00-25 (Part 3)/1

Additional information—For recommendations concerning acceptable operating forces for various types of controls see section 26. Compilations of data concerning human strength may be found in Damon et al. (1966, Ch 3) and van Cott and Kinkade (1972, Ch 11). The biomechanics of strength is discussed in Singleton (1982, Ch 3). Pheasant (1986) has sections on both hand tools and lifting and handling tasks; the latter are also reviewed in NIOSH (1981) and Troup and Edwards (1985).

Figure 7.2 Acceptable one-handed lifting forces in the standing position   From DEF STAN 00-25 (Part 3)/1

Part two
Environment

The sections which follow are mainly concerned with various forms of *energy*—heat, light, sound, etc. We shall not only consider the *physical* units in which these forms of energy are measured and the levels or intensities considered to be *physiologically* compatible with health and safety, but also certain *psychological* responses to environmental stimuli, and the narrower range of conditions compatible with a *subjective* state of *comfort*. Broadly speaking these define an optimally designed physical environment and in general, both need to be considered in the context of the *task* which people will undertake in the environment concerned. We shall not, however, deal with the engineering problems of environmental control or with the technical means by which an ergonomically satisfactory environment is to be achieved.

Certain important environmental factors have been omitted on the somewhat arbitrary grounds that they are not generally considered to fall within the subject area of ergonomics (hazards from dust, toxic chemicals, and radiation, etc.), or that they are only of interest to a narrow range of specialists (high altitude, the under sea environment, etc.).

Section 8 The thermal environment

Heat exchanges between the human body and its environment may be summarized by the *heat balance equation*:

$$M \pm C \pm K \pm R - E = S$$

Where:

M is the heat generated by the body's metabolic processes (particularly physical work);

C is the heat lost or gained by conduction (through solid media);

K is the heat lost or gained by convection (by air currents);

R is the heat lost or gained by radiation;

E is the heat lost by the evaporation of sweat;

S is the total quantity of heat lost or gained by the tissues of the body.

When $S = 0$, the body is in thermal equilibrium and body temperature remains steady at the 'normal' level of approximately $37\,°C$.

The body's regulatory mechanisms are such that thermal equilibrium can be maintained in a wide range of environmental conditions. Failure to do so results in hyperpyrexia and heat stroke (if body temperature rises) or hypothermia (if it falls), either of which may, in the extreme, be fatal. A much narrower range of climatic conditions is compatible with *thermal comfort*—the subjective state of well-being which results when thermal equilibrium can be maintained without difficulty.

Heat stress may be defined as the loading which circumstances impose upon the thermoregulatory mechanisms of the human body. The degree of heat stress is a function of the following factors:

- physical work load;
- the thermal insulation of clothing;
- air temperature;
- thermal radiation from nearby surfaces;
- air humidity;
- air speed.

The same factors determine *thermal comfort*.

8.1 Units and measurements

Ambient temperatures are correctly specified in degrees Celsius (°C) commonly called degrees Centigrade. Heat energy is measured in joules (J) hence the rate of heat flow or heat production is given in watts (W). 1 watt = 1 joule/sec; 1 joule = 2.389 kilocalories (non-SI unit).

Although *air temperature* (t_a) may be properly measured with any conventional thermometer, it does not provide a sufficient description of the thermal environment. The literature contains references to many special measuring instruments and many composite indices such as the various scales of *effective temperature* (ET). The general aim of all these endeavours is to provide a single figure which adequately expresses the heat stress to which a person is exposed.

The *natural wet bulb temperature* (t_{nw}) is measured using a thermometer which is surrounded by a wetted wick—it is therefore a function of humidity as well as temperature *per se*. The *globe temperature* (t_g) is measured with a thermometer which is enclosed in a matt black sphere—it is a simple index of the radiant heat load on the body. This may be more precisely specified as a *mean radiant temperature* (t_r) the measurement of which is too complex to go into here. These and other measurements are described in detail in ISO 7726.

The dampness of the air is usually expressed in terms of its *relative humidity* (RH), which is approximately equal to the ratio of the moisture content of the air to that of saturated air at the same temperature. An increase in humidity leads to an increase in thermal stress by reducing factor E in the heat balance equation.

The above measurements may be combined to give various scales of effective temperature (ET). The original or 'old' scale was a composite of air temperature, wet bulb temperature, and windspeed (generally calculated from a nomogram). At 100 % RH, wet bulb temperature, air temperature and effective temperature (ET) are all equal. Air temperature was subsequently replaced by globe temperature, to give the *corrected effective temperature scale* (CET).

The 'new' effective temperature or *subjective temperature* scale (designated ET*) has now superseded the others. ET* is equal to air temperature when RH = 50 %; when the air movement is 0.1 m/s (typical for indoor conditions); and when the walls of the room are at the same temperature as the air. Hence ET* describes the subjective thermal sensations of any environment in terms of the equivalent air temperature under 'normal' (or ideal) indoor conditions. Table 8.1 gives typical responses of people to a variety of effective temperatures. Whenever you see an effective temperature quoted you should take care to establish which scale is being used.

Metabolic rate (M) may be determined by measurements of a person's oxygen consumption or from reference tables. It is specified in watts or in watts per square metre of body surface area. (Average body surface is assumed to be 1.8 m².) Table 8.2 shows typical metabolic rates for a range of activities.

Metabolic rate is occasionally specified in a special unit, the *met* (= 58 W/m²).

Table 8.1 Typical responses to effective temperature (ET*)

°F	°C	
110	43	Just tolerable for brief periods
90	32	Upper limit of reasonable tolerance
80	26	Extremely fatiguing to work in. Performance deteriorates badly and people complain a lot
78	25	Optimal for bathing, showering. Sleep is disturbed
75	24	People feel warm, lethargic and sleepy. Optimal for unclothed people
72	22	Most comfortable year-round indoor temperature for sedentary people
70	21	Optimum for performance of mental work
64	18	Physically inactive people begin to shiver. Active people are comfortable
60	16	Manual dexterity impaired (stiffness and numbness of fingers)
50	10	Lower limit of reasonable tolerance
32	0	Risk of frost-bite to exposed flesh

Notes

These figures are a rough guide only and should not be used for design purposes. Effective temperature (ET*) is equal to air temperature when relative humidity is 50 %, air flow is small and radiant heat is negligible.

Compiled with reference to Woodson (1981), Bennett (1977), Grandjean (1981), etc.

The thermal insulation (resistance) of clothing is specified either in physical units (m² °C/W) or else (more commonly) in a special dimensionless unit, the *clo* (1 clo = 0.155 m² °C/W). Thermal resistances of some male clothing ensembles are given in table 8.3. Outdoor clothing extends to 4 clo for specially designed polar suits. Down sleeping bags may have a thermal resistance of up to 6 clo.

Table 8.2 Classification of levels of metabolic rate

Class	Metabolic rate range, M		Value to be used for calculation of mean metabolic rate		Examples
	related to a unit skin surface area W/m^2	for a mean skin surface area of 1.8 m^2 W	W/m^2	W	
0 Resting	$M \leqslant 65$	$M \leqslant 117$	65	117	Resting
1 Low metabolic rate	$65 < M \leqslant 130$	$117 < M \leqslant 234$	100	180	**Sitting at ease:** light manual work (writing, typing, drawing, sewing, book-keeping); hand and arm work (small bench tools, inspection, assembly or sorting of light materials); arm and leg work (driving vehicle in normal conditions, operating foot switch or pedal). **Standing:** drill (small parts); milling machine (small parts); coil winding; small armature winding; machining with low-power tools; casual walking (speed up to 3.5 km/h).
2 Moderate metabolic rate	$130 < M \leqslant 200$	$234 < M \leqslant 360$	165	297	Sustained hand and arm work (hammering in nails, filing); arm and leg work (off-road operation of lorries, tractors or construction equipment); arm and trunk work (work with pneumatic hammer, tractor assembly, plastering, intermittent handling of moderately heavy material, weeding, hoeing, picking fruit or vegetables); pushing or pulling light-weight carts or wheelbarrows; walking at a speed of 3.5 to 5.5 km/h; forging.
3 High metabolic rate	$200 < M \leqslant 260$	$360 < M \leqslant 468$	230	414	Intense arm and trunk work; carrying heavy material; shovelling; sledge hammer work; sawing, planing or chiselling hard wood; hand mowing; digging; walking at a speed of 5.5 to 7 km/h. Pushing or pulling heavily loaded handcarts or wheelbarrows; chipping castings; concrete block laying.
4 Very high metabolic rate	$M < 260$	$M < 468$	290	522	Very intense activity at fast to maximum pace; working with an axe; intense shovelling or digging; climbing stairs, ramp or ladder; walking quickly with small steps, running, walking at a speed greater than 7 km/h.

From ISO 7243

Table 8.3 Values of typical clothing ensembles

Clothing ensemble	I_{cl}	
	$(m^2 \cdot {}^\circ C/W)$	(clo)
Nude	0	0
Shorts	0.015	0.1
Typical tropical clothing ensemble: briefs, shorts, open-neck shirt with short sleeves, light socks and sandals	0.045	0.3
Light summer clothing: briefs, long light-weight trousers, open-neck shirt with short sleeves, light socks and shoes	0.08	0.5
Light working ensemble: light underwear, cotton work shirt with long sleeves, work trousers, woollen socks and shoes	0.11	0.7
Typical indoor winter clothing ensemble: underwear, shirt with long sleeves, trousers, jacket or sweater with long sleeves, heavy socks and shoes	0.16	1.0
Heavy traditional European business suit: cotton underwear with long legs and sleeves, shirt, suit including trousers, jacket and waistcoat, woollen socks and heavy shoes	0.23	1.5

From ISO 7730

8.2 Heat stress—the WBGT index

The currently favoured index of heat stress is the wet bulb globe temperature (WBGT) index as described in ISO 7243.

Inside buildings, and outside buildings without solar load:
  WBGT index $= 0.7t_{nw} + 0.3t_g$

Outside buildings, with solar load:
  WBGT index $= 0.7t_{nw} + 0.2t_g + 0.1t_a$
(see previous section for meanings of terms)

Table 8.4 shows *reference values* of WBGT based on a maximal permissible rectal temperature of 38 °C for a physically fit person wearing a 0.6 clo clothing ensemble. 'If these values are exceeded, it is necessary to reduce directly the heat stress at the work place ... or to carry out a more detailed analysis of the heat stress in accordance with more elaborate methods' (ISO 7243).

An alternative (and presumably more sophisticated) method of calculating heat stress, based on predicted sweat rate, is the subject of a standard which is currently at the draft stage (ISO 7933).

Table 8.4 Reference value of the WBGT heat stress index

Metabolic rate class	Metabolic rate, M		Reference value of WBGT			
	Related to a unit skin surface area W/m^2	Total (for a mean skin surface area of 1.8 m^2) W	Person acclimatized to heat °C		Person not acclimatized to heat °C	
0 (resting)	$M \leqslant 65$	$M \leqslant 117$	33		32	
1	$65 < M \leqslant 130$	$117 < M \leqslant 234$	30		29	
2	$130 < M \leqslant 200$	$234 < M \leqslant 360$	28		26	
3	$200 < M \leqslant 260$	$360 < M \leqslant 468$	No sensible air movement 25	Sensible air movement 26	No sensible air movement 22	Sensible air movement 23
4	$M > 260$	$M > 468$	23	25	18	20

From ISO 7243

8.3 Cold Stress

The most serious risks associated with cold stress are frost-bite and hypothermia.

Frost-bite occurs when the flesh is exposed to sub-zero temperatures. Hypothermia (drop in body temperature) will not usually be a risk for the physically active person (except in very severe environments). For inactive (and possibly malnourished) elderly people it constitutes a serious hazard.

Manual dexterity deteriorates at temperatures below 16 °C (approximately) and is severely impaired at 13 °C (owing to numbness, stiffness and weakness of the fingers).

Stressfully cold working environments are less commonly encountered than stressfully hot ones. Cold stress indices are correspondingly less sophisticated. The cooling power of an environment is commonly expressed on the *windchill scale*:

$$K_o = (10 \sqrt{V} + 10.45 - V)(33 - T_a)$$

where

K_o is the windchill factor

V is the air speed (m/s)

T_a is the air temperature (°C).

(The units of K_o as defined above are kcal/m²/h—to convert to SI units, W/m², multipy by 1.162). K_o only provides an approximate index of the rate of cooling of an exposed person—since the original experiments upon which it was based were conducted on containers of water. Table 8.5 provides a rough guide to its interpretation (Parker and West 1973).

Table 8.5 Interpretation of windchill index (K_o)

K_o	Interpretation
<90	Hot
90 to 150	Warm
150 to 300	Pleasant
300 to 500	Cool
500 to 700	Very cool
700 to 900	Cold
900 to 1100	Very cold
1100 to 1300	Bitterly cold
>1300	Exposed flesh freezes
>1650	Exposed flesh freezes in one minute
>2150	Exposed flesh freezes in 30 seconds

From Parker and West (1973)

8.4 UK statutory requirements

Both the Factories Act 1961 and the Offices, Shops and Railway Premises Act 1963 set a lower limit to the temperature which is allowable in the working environment for people engaged in activities which do not demand strenuous physical efforts. In the former case the limit is specified as 60 °F and in the latter as '16 °C (which is equivalent to 60.8 °Fahrenheit)'. In both cases the first hour of work is excluded.

The Fuel and Electricity (Heating) (Control) (Amendment) Order 1980 (SI No 1013) requires that premises must not be heated by the use of electricity or fuel to a temperature of more than 19 °C.

8.5 Thermal comfort—the Fanger/ISO index

Thermal comfort is defined in ISO 7730 as 'that condition of mind which expresses satisfaction with the thermal environment'. ISO 7730 is based on the methodology of Fanger (1973) which is widely regarded as having superseded previous alternatives. The Fanger/ISO method is too complex to present in detail here. It is based on a lengthy equation which relates metabolic rate, clothing and various environmental factors to the subjective feelings of comfort (or otherwise) of a typical group of people. (The equation itself is based partly on theoretical considerations and partly an experimental study of more than 1300 subjects.) For any combination of work/clothing/environment it is possible to calculate two indices: the *predicted mean vote* (PMV) on a particular comfort rating scale and the *predicted percentage* (of people) who would be *dissatisfied* (PPD). Owing to human variability it is not possible for PPD to be reduced below 5%. The specialist reader should refer to ISO 7730 or Fanger (1973) for further details.

Thermal comfort—simplified guidelines

The following notes are intended for the non-specialist. They are based on Fanger (1973), Grandjean (1981), Clark and Corlett (1984) and ISO 7730. The guidelines apply to *sedentary workers*, wearing indoor garments appropriate to the season, (1 clo in winter, 0.5 clo in summer):

- ISO 7730 recommends temperatures of 22 ± 2°C in winter and 24.5 ± 1.5°C in summer. (Strictly speaking these are averages of air temperature and mean radiant temperature.) Fanger's research, on which this was based, was conducted in the USA. British and European sources tend to recommend lower figures—a comfort range of 19°C to 22°C would be typical. Grandjean (who is Swiss) recommends a winter temperature of 21°C and states that summer temperatures of 20°C to 24°C are 'comfortable'. Fanger considers that apparent national differences are in fact due to customary differences in clothing. A sensible (and pragmatic) compromise might be to say that there is little point in expending energy to heat a naturally cool environment above 20°C or to cool a naturally hot one below 24°C.

- The temperatures of walls and other adjacent surfaces should not differ from air temperature by more than 3 ± 3°C, *neither should the air temperature at head and foot levels*. (For rooms with large windows this, in winter, is something of a counsel of perfection.)

- A relative humidity of 40% to 50% is ideal—however, the effect of humidity on comfort is relatively small within the normal temperature range. A room feels 'stuffy' at an RH greater than 80% at 18°C or 60% at 24°C. In modern air-conditioned environments, excessively dry air (RH < 30%) is a major problem—it leads to dessication of the mucous membranes and chronic irritation of the nasal and bronchial passages (Grandjean 1981). It also causes electrostatic nuisance.

- Air movements of more than 0.15 m/s in winter or 0.25 m/s in summer are uncomfortably draughty for sedentary people.

- Manual workers require lower air temperatures and higher air movements than sedentary workers. Temperatures ranging from 19°C down to 15°C are desirable depending on physical workload.

8.6 Ventilation

Indoor environments must be adequately ventilated (i.e. supplied with outdoor 'fresh' air) in order to:

- maintain the correct balance of respiratory gases (oxygen, carbon dioxide);

- remove or dilute unpleasant odours, tobacco smoke and potentially hazardous chemical or biological contaminants;

● remove excess heat.

Principles of ventilation are discussed in BS 5925, from which a few extracts follow.

The air flow required to reduce the odour of sedentary adults to an acceptable level is shown in figure 8.1 as a function of the per capita allocation of space.

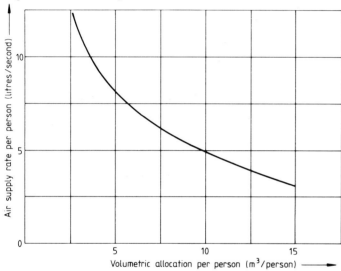

Figure 8.1 Air supply rate for odour removal
From BS 5925

The average smoker consumes 1.3 cigarettes per hour. This requires a fresh air rate of 7 L/s per smoker. Cigarette smoke is extremely unpleasant for non-smokers—furthermore, many authorities now believe that 'passive smoking' (the consumption of other people's smoke) carries a measurable health risk.

Table 8.6 lists recommended outside air supply rates taking into account the likely density of occupation and the type and amount of smoking.

Table 8.6 Recommended outdoor air supply rates for air-conditioned spaces

Reproduced here and in BS 5925 : 1980 from the CIBS Guide by permission of the Chartered Institution of Building Services

Type of space	Smoking	Outdoor air supply		
		Recommended	Minimum (take greater of the two)	
		Per person	Per person	Per m² floor area
		litres/s	litres/s	litres/s
Factories*†	None			0.8
Offices (open plan)	Some			1.3
Shops and stores	Some	8	5	3.0
Theatres*	Some			—
Dance halls*	Some			—
Hotel bedrooms†	Heavy			1.7
Laboratories†	Some			—
Offices (private)	Heavy	12	8	1.3
Residences (average)	Heavy			—
Restaurants (cafeteria)†‡	Some			—
Cocktail bars	Heavy			—
Conference rooms (average)	Some			—
Residences (luxury)	Heavy	18	12	—
Restaurants (dining rooms)†	Heavy			—
Board rooms, executive offices and conference rooms	Very heavy	25	18	6.0
Corridors	A per capita basis is not appropriate to these spaces			1.3
Kitchens (domestic)†				10.0
Kitchens (restaurant)†				20.0
Toilets*				10.0

*See statutory requirements and local bye-laws.
†Rate of extraction may be overriding factor.
‡Where queueing occurs in space, seating capacity may not be appropriate total occupancy.
Notes 1. For hospital wards and operating theatres see DHSS Building Notes.
      2. Outdoor air supply rates given take account of likely density of occupation and type and amount of smoking.

8.7 Hot surfaces

Living human tissue is burned when its temperature reaches 43 °C. Any object at this temperature or over coming in contact with the skin will cause a sensation of warmth followed by discomfort, pain and ultimately a burn. The rate at which these stages progress depends on the temperature of the object, certain physical properties of the material from which it is made (thermal conductivity, density, specific heat) and other factors. These matters are discussed in a BSI published document (PD 6504). Figures 8.2 and 8.3 show the time taken to reach the thresholds of discomfort and pain when the palm and fingertip respectively were held in contact with a hot object. (Note that the palm is slightly more resistant to burning than other parts of the body because it has a thicker layer of skin.) Figure 8.4 shows the time taken to cause a burn when a heated brass object was held against the skin (of the human forearm or animal skin of similar thickness).

It is not easy to convert these data into specific guidelines concerning product design. BS 4086 gives recommendations concerning the maximum temperatures of the 'non-working surfaces' of domestic heated equipment; but these have been the object of some controversy and some people consider them to be too high. The UK Government is at present drafting a regulation on the surface temperature of cookers which will probably necessitate the revision of BS 4086.

Additional information—The thermal environment in general is discussed in Grandjean (1981, Ch 17), Singleton (1982, Ch 5) and Oborne (1981, Ch 11). The definitive treatment of thermal comfort is Fanger (1973).

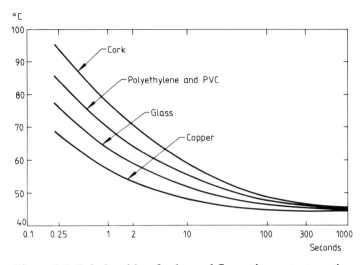

Figure 8.2 Relationship of palm and fingertip contact causing discomfort with time and temperature   From PD 6504

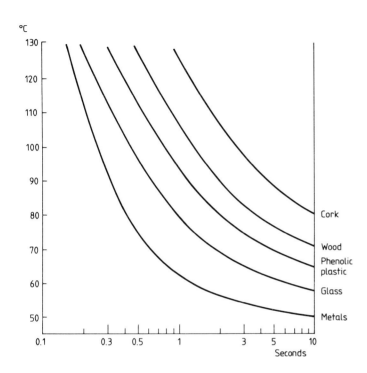

Figure 8.3 Relationship of palm and fingertip contact causing pain with time and temperature   From PD 6504

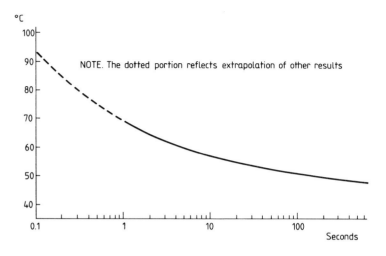

Figure 8.4 Onset of burning in the skin after contact for various times with a brass block at various constant temperatures
From PD 6504

Section 9 Electric shock

The consequences of an electric shock depend upon the current passing through the body. The following levels are approximate. A current of one milliampere (mA) is just at the threshold of sensation. A shock of 3 mA to 10 mA causes pain but no muscle spasm. At levels greater than about 10 mA muscle spasm may cause the victim to have difficulty in letting go of the live object. In the 20 mA to 50 mA range pain and spasm are severe and breathing becomes difficult. Above about 50 mA there is an increasing risk of ventricular fibrillation—that is, the heart may stop beating and the outcome may be fatal.

A publication of the International Electrotechnical Commission (IEC 479) discusses these effects in greater detail. The current which flows is dependent upon the touch voltage (in volts, V) and the body resistance (in ohms, Ω). For the human body the resistance is itself dependent upon the voltage, according to the following relationship:

Touch voltage (V)	Body resistance (Ω)
25	2 500
50	2 000
250	1 000
asymptotic value	650

From IEC 479

These figures apply to direct current (d.c.) and alternating current (a.c.) up to 100 Hz; they assume that current is flowing from hand to hand or from hand to foot and that the skin is normally moist.

Figure 9.1 shows the likely effects on human beings of passing an alternating current (50 Hz to 60 Hz) of I_B mA (rms) for a period of t milliseconds. Zone 1 is generally below threshold; in zone 2 reaction may occur but 'usually no pathologically dangerous effects are to be expected'. Zones 3 and 4 are increasingly dangerous. There is a steady transition between zones. IEC 479 also contains a similar chart for direct current.

Data of this kind must not be used in isolation when considering the safety of electrical products. Other factors to take into account may include the probability of faults, the possibility of the user touching a live part, the relation between the touch voltage and the fault voltage, etc. A further consideration of these matters is to be found in BS 3456.

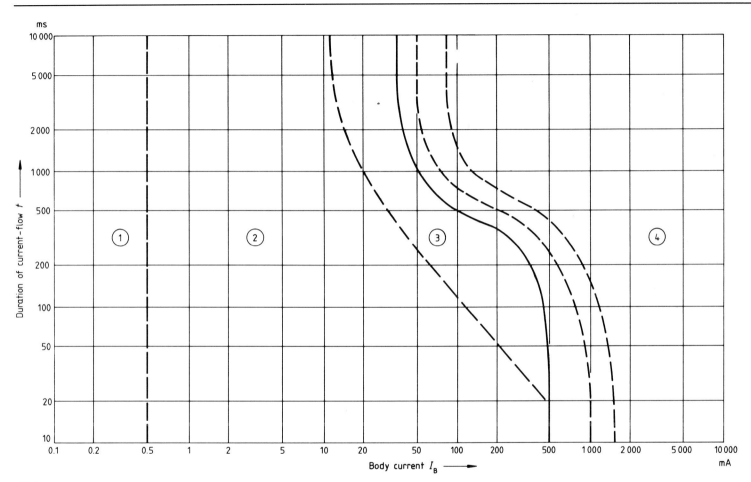

Notes.
1. As regards ventricular fibrillation, this figure relates to the effects of current which flows in the path 'left hand to feet'. For other current paths, see the complete standard.
2. The point 500 mA/100 ms corresponds to a fibrillation probability in the order of 0.14%.

Figure 9.1 Time/current zones of effects of a.c. currents (15 Hz to 100 Hz) on persons
From IEC 479-1

Section 10 Light

Light is a form of electromagnetic radiation. The human eye responds to wavelengths extending from 380 nm at the violet end of the visible spectrum to 780 nm at the red (1 nm = 10^{-9} m). The peak sensitivity of the eye is in the middle (green) part of this range.

10.1 Units and definitions

The basic unit for *luminous intensity* of a light source (that is, the energy it emits per unit time) is the *candela* (cd). The exact definition of this unit need not concern us, but for convenience we could think of it as the output of a standard candle, which is radiating light equally in all directions. The energy flow in any particular direction is known as the *luminous flux*. The *lumen* (lm) is the luminous flux emitted through a solid angle of one steradian (sr) by a one candela light source. (The steradian is the solid angle which, having its vertex in the centre of a sphere, cuts off an area of the surface of the sphere equal to that of a square with sides of length equal to the radius of the sphere.)

The quantity of light *falling on a surface* is known as its *illumination* (or more correctly, its *illuminance*). Its unit is the *lux* (lx). 1 lx = 1 lm/m². (Hence a one candela source placed at the centre of a sphere of 1m radius will give its inner surface 1 lx of illumination.)

The *luminance* of an object is the quantity of light *coming from* its surface (per unit area). It is thus the physical correlate of the subjective sensation of *brightness*. The SI unit of luminance is the cd/m². Table 10.1 shows the luminances of a variety of objects and sources. Illumination and luminance are related by a dimensionless quantity called *reflectance* (which is the proportion of light incident upon a surface which is reflected back to an observer). This relation defines a non-SI unit of luminance called the apostilb (asb), hence:

Table 10.1 Typical values for luminance levels

cd/m²

Scale	Value	Description
10^9	1.4×10^9	Sun viewed from earth
10^8	2.5×10^8	Atomic bomb viewed from 6 km
10^7		
10^6		
10^5	1.7×10^5	100 W frosted light bulb
	2.8×10^4	Snow at noon
10^4	6.4×10^3	Average sky on a clear day
10^3	1.6×10^3	Average sky on a cloudy day
10^2		
	6.4×10^1	White paper in good reading light
10^1	3.2×10^1	TV screen
	2.5×10^0	Snow in full moon
10^0		
10^{-1}	6.4×10^{-2}	Lower limit for useful colour vision
	3.2×10^{-2}	Upper limit for dark-adapted vision
10^{-2}		
10^{-3}		
10^{-4}		
	3.2×10^{-5}	Moonless night sky; absolute threshold for dark-adapted eye
10^{-5}		
	3×10^{-6}	Interstellar space
10^{-6}		

Data from Parker and West (1973) and Bennett (1977)

luminance (asb) = illuminance (lux) x reflectance
(1 asb = $1/\pi$ cd/m²).

Table 10.2 shows the approximate reflectances of some common surfaces.

Adaptation

The human eye has evolved in such a way that its sensitivity is continually *adapted* to match the prevailing light conditions—hence, we can see perfectly well in both daylight and moonlight although the overall levels of illumination differ by a factor of about 10^5. The time required for complete *dark adaptation* (when we move from a bright environment into a dark one) is around 30 minutes to 40 minutes. The dark adapted eye is not sensitive to colour difference. The reverse process, *light adaptation*, is very much more rapid—most of it occurs within the first second of exposure to a bright light and it is completed in about two minutes.

An important consequence of the above is that the *apparent brightness* of an object or a light source is dependent not only upon its luminance (that is, its physical 'brightness') but also on the luminance of the background against which it is seen—which governs the level of adaptation of the eye. Hence, car headlights which are blindingly bright at night are scarcely noticeable during the day.

Table 10.2 Approximate reflectance values of some common surfaces

Surface	Reflectance
	%
Fresh white plaster	95
White paint; white tiles or good quality white paper	85
White plastic; light grey or cream paint; medium quality white paper; bright brass or aluminium	75
Medium yellow, pastel blue, pink or green paint	65
Newsprint; concrete; medium grey, pink or orange paint	55
Plain white wood; powdered chalk	45
Dark grey paint	30
Bright steel	25
Good quality printers' ink	15
Mahogany; dark blue, brown, or deep red paint	12
Matt black paper	5

From Murrell (1969), Grandjean (1981), Woodson and Conover (1964).

10.2 Lighting design

The principal ergonomic objectives in designing the lighting of an indoor space are:

- to provide adequate illumination for the performance of the range of tasks associated with the space;
- to avoid glare;
- to enhance the aesthetic qualities of the environment.

(There will, of course, be various engineering or technical objectives also—such as the minimization of energy expenditure, etc.—but these are not our present concern.)

UK statutory requirements

Both the Factories Act 1961 and the Offices, Shops and Railway Premises Act 1963 require the provision of 'sufficient and suitable lighting, whether natural or artificial'. Advice concerning the interpretation of this requirement is given in HSE (1976) which includes a table of minimum levels of illumination which 'in the opinion of the Department of Employment and Productivity' are likely to meet the obligations of the Offices, Shops and Railway Premises Act. It is pointed out however that the decision as to whether a given lighting scheme is 'sufficient and suitable' ultimately rests with the relevant statutory authorities.

Task illumination

BS 8206: Part 1 recommends values of *standard service illuminance* as quoted in table 10.3. This is the illuminance required, in the plane of a task, under typical conditions. When the situation is not typical, the illuminance can be modified, according to the flow chart in table 10.4, to give the *design service illuminance*.

Table 10.5 shows specific task illumination requirements as given in MIL-STD-1472C. Levels are specified either 'on the task' or on a horizontal plane 780 mm from the floor. The 'minimum' values given in the table are in all cases greater than equivalent figures given in HSE (1976). The 'recommended' values given in the table are generally somewhat higher than the 'standard service values' given in the CIBS code (CIBS 1984). For recommendations concerning the lighting of computer workstations, see section 17.2.

Colour of light sources

Light sources differ in their spectral characteristics and hence in the quality of their *apparent colour* and the accuracy with which they *render* the colour of illuminated surfaces. BS 8206: Part 1 deals briefly with these matters. In general, lamps with differing apparent colours should not be used haphazardly in the same room. In areas with an illuminance of less than 300 lx a 'warm' or 'intermediate' light source is preferred, since 'cold' lamps give a gloomy appearance. Light sources with good colour rendering properties make surfaces appear more colourful and may be critical in some tasks.

Table 10.3 Recommended values of standard service illuminance

Standard service illuminance (lx)	Characteristics of the activity/interior	Representative activities/interiors
50	Interiors visited rarely with visual tasks confined to movement and casual seeing without perception of detail	Walkways, cable tunnels
100	Interiors visited occasionally with visual tasks confined to movement and casual seeing calling for only limited perception of detail	Bulk stores, corridors
150	Interiors visited occasionally with visual tasks requiring some perception of detail Interiors visited occasionally but involving some risk to people, plant or product	Churches Loading bays
200	Continuously occupied interiors, visual tasks not requiring any perception of detail	Monitoring automatic processes in manufacture, turbine halls
300	Continuously occupied interiors, visual tasks moderately easy, i.e. details to be seen are large and/or of high contrast	Lecture theatres, packing goods, rough sawing
500	Visual tasks moderately difficult, i.e. details to be seen are of moderate size and may be of low contrast. Also colour judgement may be required	General offices, kitchens, laboratories
750	Visual tasks difficult, i.e. details to be seen are small and of low contrast. Also good colour judgement may be required	Drawing offices, ceramic decoration
1000	Visual tasks very difficult, i.e. details to be seen are very small and may be of very low contrast. Also accurate colour judgements may be required	Electronic component assembly, gauge and tool rooms, retouching paintwork
1500	Visual tasks extremely difficult, i.e. details to be seen extremely small and of low contrast. Visual aids may be of advantage	Inspection of graphic reproduction, hand tailoring
2000	Visual tasks exceptionally difficult, i.e. details to be seen exceptionally small and of very low contrast. Visual aids will be of advantage	Assembly of minute mechanisms, finished fabric inspection

From BS 8206: Part 1

Table 10.4 Flow chart for obtaining the design service illuminance from the standard service illuminance

Standard service illuminance (lx)	Are the task details unusually difficult to see?	Are the task details unusually easy to see?*†	Is the task done for an unusually short time?*†	Is the task done for an unusually long time?*†	Is visual impairment widespread among those doing the work?‡	Do errors have unusually serious consequences for people, plant or product?	Design service illuminance (lx)§‖

* The standard service illuminances recommended in the schedule are based on tasks which are representative of their type in the detail that has to be seen and the time for which the task has to be done. These steps in the flow chart allow for departures from these assumed conditions.

† The standard service illuminance of 200 lx is provided as an amenity for continuously occupied interiors, even when perception of task detail is not required.

‡ If the cause of visual impairment is dirty or scratched spectacles, safety glasses, safety screens, etc., it may be more effective to clean and/or replace these items rather than change the lighting. If safety screens are acting as a source of veiling reflections, then the lighting/task/worker geometry should be rearranged.

§ If the design service illuminance is more than two steps on the illuminance scale above the standard service illuminance, consideration should be given to whether the changes in the task details, the organization of the work or the people doing the work are more appropriate than changing the lighting.

‖ For the design service illuminance of 1500 lx or 2000 lx, local lighting supplemented by optical aids should be considered.

From BS 8206: Part 1

Table 10.5 Specific task illumination requirements

Task or environment	Illumination (lx)	
	Recommended	Minimum
Emergency lighting		30
Warehouse storage	110	55
Hallways; stairways; corridors; service areas	215	110
Dials; meters; console surfaces; switchboards	540	325
Office work (general)	755	540
Business machine operation	1075	540
Benchwork; assembly work; inspection tasks		
— rough or coarse	540	325
— medium	810	540
— fine	1075	810
— extra fine or precise	3230	2155
Reading		
— large print	325	110
— newsprint	540	325
— handwritten (in pencil), or small type, or prolonged reading	755	540

From MIL-STD-1472C

Glare

The presence in the visual field of an excessively bright object or an excessive degree of brightness contrast leads to the unpleasant visual sensation known as *glare* (or 'dazzle').

Glare may be *direct* (as from an unshaded light source) or *reflected* from a polished or glossy surface (such as a VDU screen). The latter is sometimes called *specular glare*. Modest degrees of glare cause visual *discomfort* and lead to 'eyestrain'. More intense glare causes *disability* (i.e. a decrement in performance of visual tasks). The eye tends to move towards the brightest part of the visual field (the phototropic effect).

The glare caused by a bright object is dependent on a number of factors:

- *Glare increases* with the luminance of the object and with its apparent size (i.e. the solid angle which it subtends at the eye).
- *Glare decreases* with the luminance of the background against which the object is viewed and with the distance of the object from the centre of the visual field (i.e. the angle subtended at the eye between the object and the line of sight). A bright object above the line of sight causes less glare than one below the line of sight or to the side.

These factors may be combined to give the *glare constant* of a source or the *glare index* of an environment, the calculation of which is described in Hopkinson and Collins (1970) and in CIBS (1984).

The following guidelines for the design of lighting which, if they do not eliminate glare altogether, should at least reduce it to acceptable levels. They are compiled from the ergonomics literature in general and Grandjean (1981) in particular.

- It is usually advantageous for demanding visual tasks to have high contrast (e.g. black print on white paper). Other than this the following contrast levels (i.e. ratios of luminance) should not be exceeded:

—between sizeable areas near the line of sight, 3:1;
—between the centre of the visual area and its periphery or between objects in its periphery, 10:1;
—between light sources and their surrounds, 20:1.

- Avoid placing light sources within 60° of the line of sight when the eyes are in their working position or within 30° of a horizontal line of sight. If this cannot be achieved light sources should be carefully shielded. Fluorescent tubes should be at right angles to the most common direction of vision.

- In general, several small luminaires are better than one or two large ones and diffuse lighting reflected from the walls and ceiling is better than direct lighting.

- Working equipment and other objects in the centre of the visual field should have matt surfaces rather than polished ones. Where this is not possible (as on a VDU screen for example) care must be taken not to reflect windows or light sources into the user's eyes.

- Suitable values of reflectance, and relative illuminance of surfaces in a room are given in figure 10.1. Illuminances are quoted relative to the illuminance of the task which is given a value of 1.0.

- Flickering light from rotating machinery, defective fluorescent tubes, etc., is extremely stressful. Some people are disturbed by the 'invisible flicker' of fluorescent tubes; this can be reduced by using fittings in which the tubes are mounted in pairs and a phase shift is incorporated in the power supply.

Additional information—Discussions of the ergonomics of lighting may be found in Grandjean (1981, Ch 15), Oborne (1981, Ch 11) and Singleton (1982, Ch 6). Hopkinson and Collins (1970) and Boyce (1981) give very detailed accounts of the subject. CIBS (1984) represents current good practice.

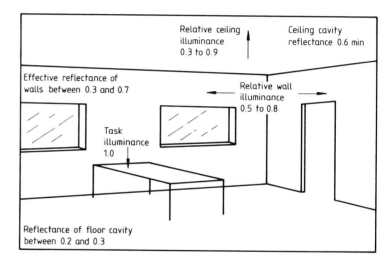

Figure 10.1 Recommended ranges of reflectance and relative illuminance for room surfaces
From BS 8206: Part 1

Section 11 Colour

The colours of the visible spectrum are red (780 nm to 627 nm wavelengths), orange (627 nm to 589 nm), yellow (589 nm to 566 nm), green (566 nm to 495 nm), blue (495 nm to 436 nm) and violet (436 nm to 380 nm). The colour purple is said to be 'extra-spectral'. Sunlight contains a mixture of all these wavelengths (together with infra-red and ultraviolet).

Solid objects reflect part of the light which falls on them (or transmit light through if they are translucent)—the remainder is absorbed. Hence, if an object reflects green light (wavelength circa 500 nm) and absorbs all others it is perceived as being 'a green object'. White objects reflect all wavelengths of light; black objects reflect none. Grey objects reflect a certain proportion of all wavelengths.

11.1 The Munsell colour system

Many systems have been proposed for describing colours. The most commonly adopted is the Munsell system which is found for example in BS 381C and BS 4800. Colours are 'located' in a three dimensional space (see figure 11.1) defined by three independent attributes called *hue, value* and *chroma*. We may draw this space as a sphere or a double cone (the colour solid) which has the spectral colours in sequence around the equator (the colour circle) with white and black at the poles and shades of grey along the axis.

Hue (which is more or less equivalent to spectral colour) is designated B, blue; BG, blue/green; G, green; GY, green/yellow; Y, yellow; YR, yellow/red; R, red; RP, red/purple; P, purple; PB, purple/blue. Each named hue may be divided into 10 numbered grades (centred on 5).

Value refers to the lightness of a colour (plotted on the vertical scale) from zero (black) via nine intervening shades of grey to 10 (white). Munsell value (V) is approximately related to reflectance (R) by the equation:

$$R\,(\%) = V\,(V\text{-}1)$$

Chroma refers to the purity or saturation of a colour (plotted on the horizontal scale) from zero for neutral greys to numbers up to 16 for highly saturated colours. (Not all hues can be this highly saturated.)

Hence, the colour designated 5R 3.5/16 has a middle red hue with a value of 3.5 (reflectance $\approx 9\,\%$) and a chroma of 16 (maximum saturation)—it is therefore a vivid 'pillar box' red. Neutral tones of grey (which have neither hue nor chroma) are designated by the letter N followed by their value.

The operation of the Munsell system is best understood by means of the following examples, all of which are from the same region of the colour circle:

  2.5 Y/R 7/6 is salmon pink;
  5 Y/R 2/4 is dark brown (a rich chocolate colour);
  2.5 Y 8/4 is light beige
  5 Y 9/14 is canary yellow

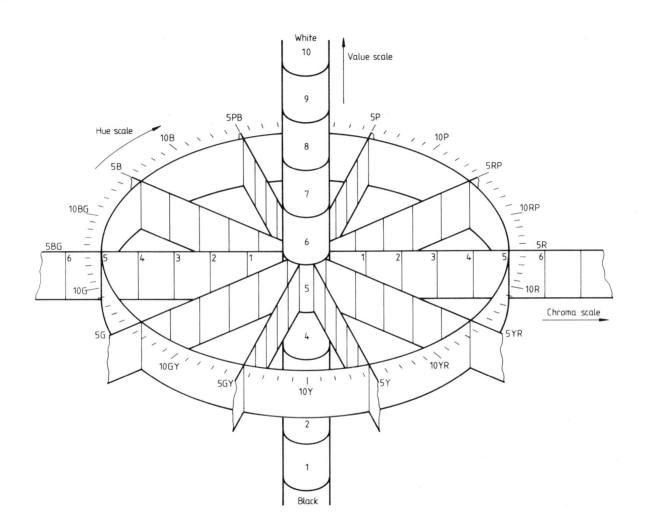

Figure 11.1 Munsell colour system

11.2 Chromaticity coordinates

An alternative to the Munsell system, which is preferred for some purposes because of its greater precision, is the International Commission on Illumination (CIE) system of chromaticity coordinates. These are determined by using a spectrophotometer and analysing its output according to the colour matching functions, known as x and y, which represent the relative sensitivity at different wavelengths of a standard observer. The results are plotted as coordinates on a *chromaticity diagram* as shown in figure 11.2 which is taken from BS 5378: Part 2.

The colours of the spectrum are located around the boundary curve (identified by wavelength on the diagram). Colours become less saturated as the central equal energy point is approached (this represents either white or black). Quoted values of chromaticity coordinates are generally supplemented by a 'luminance factor' which is almost the same thing as a value of reflectance.

11.3 The effects of colour

Conspicuity and contrast

The conspicuity of an object (that is, the readiness with which it is seen) depends on the contrast between itself and its background. Brightness contrast (i.e. differences in value or reflectance) and contrast of hue are both important. Hues which are directly opposite each other on the colour circle (known as 'complementary' hues) have the highest contrast. When viewed against a black, dark grey, brown or dark blue background, the most conspicuous colours are yellow, orange and red (in that order). In general, highly saturated colours get attention best. When pairs of highly saturated colours of similar value are placed next to each other the eye creates a shimmering white line along their boundary.

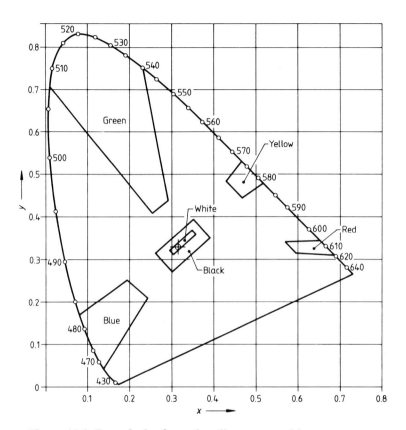

Figure 11.2 Boundaries for red, yellow, green, blue, white and black ordinary surface colours   From BS 5378: Part 2

Preferences

Much has been written about colour preferences but very little has been proved. In general, people who are presented with colour samples *in isolation* will express a preference for saturated tones (no consistent preference for specific hues has been demonstrated). However, these preferences will not generally be maintained when colours are used *in context*. Saturated colours may be considered 'oppressive', 'brash' or 'vulgar' when used for decorative purposes. Colour preferences are very much a matter of fashion—last year's tasteful avocado will look naff next year.

There is a widely held principle that dissimilar (complementary) colours form compatible combinations whereas similar colours do not. There is little evidence that people's colour preferences actually work this way—in fact people commonly express a preference for colour combinations which contradict the 'rule'.

Other effects

In general, red objects are perceived as nearer than blue ones—but this phenomenon has been shown to have little or no effect upon the apparent size of a room. It is generally said that red is a 'warm' colour and blue is a 'cool' one—but it has been shown that this has little or no effect upon subjective temperature or thermal comfort (Bennett, 1977).

There is fairly general agreement that reds, oranges and yellows are positive and stimulating; that greens and blues are soothing and relaxing; and that dull grey environments are depressing. Aside from these, the so-called 'psychological' effects of colour are largely non-existent and the literature on this subject is often silly.

Standard uses of colour

Numerous British Standards deal with recommended colours for specific products or circumstances. These include:

BS 1319 Medical gas cylinders, valves and yoke connections
BS 1710 Identification of pipelines and services
BS 5252 Framework for colour coordination for building purposes
BS 5423 Portable fire extinguishers
BS 5890 Choice of colours to be used for the marking of capacitors and resistors

Others may be found in the BSI Catalogue. See also section 26.

Section 12 Vibration

The motion of a vibrating body could in principle be described in terms of its frequency (the number of cycles of motion per unit time) and its amplitude (the distance it is displaced from its resting position in each cycle of motion). In practice, the latter is usually replaced by the body's *acceleration* measured in metres per second per second (m/s^2) or in multiples of g which is the acceleration due to gravity $9.81 m/s^2$. Acceleration is usually specified in terms of its *root mean squared* (rms) value. In common with all physical objects, the human body (and its constituent parts) has a natural frequency of vibration at which it exhibits the phenomenon of *resonance* (that is, an externally imposed vibration will have the greatest mechanical effect).

12.1 Whole body vibration

Vibration may be sensed, via nerve endings in one part of the body or another, at frequencies ranging from 10^{-1} to 10^5 Hz. If the intensity (acceleration) is sufficient, frequencies from 0.1 Hz to 20 Hz will cause people to feel unstable and to have difficulty in balancing. Motion sickness occurs at frequencies of less than about 0.6 Hz. The trunk and its parts (including the spine) resonate at between 4 Hz and 10 Hz—this may cause chest pain, abdominal pain, difficulty in breathing and damage to the spine or the gastrointestinal organs (stomach, bowels, etc.).

The head and neck resonate at frequencies around 30 Hz. The eyeball resonates at 60 Hz to 100 Hz, causing blurred vision. Between 10 Hz and 18 Hz there is an urge to urinate and at frequencies between 13 Hz and 20 Hz speech is disturbed and the voice acquires a vibrato effect.

The frequency-dependent effects of whole-body vibration may be characterized by measurements of a quantity called *mechanical*

impedance which is the ratio of force to velocity at a given frequency (see ISO 5982).

Whole-body vibration is described with respect to three axes which in principle meet at the heart: the x axis from back to chest; the y axis from side to side; and the z axis from feet (or buttocks) to head (see figure 12.1).

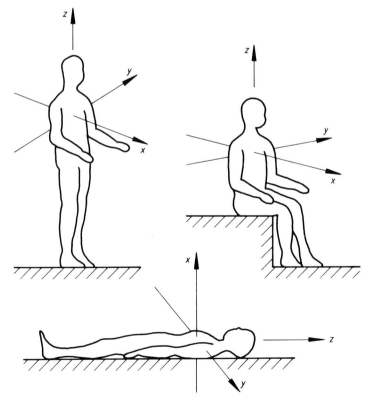

Figure 12.1 Directions of basicentric coordinate systems for mechanical vibrations influencing humans From ISO 2631/1

ISO 2631 (which is technically equivalent to British Standard draft for development DD 32) specifies limits to vibration, in the 1 Hz to 80 Hz range of frequencies, at three different levels.

1 *The fatigue-decreased proficiency boundary* 'beyond which exposure to vibration can be regarded as carrying a significant risk of impaired working efficiency in many kinds of tasks, particularly those in which time-dependent effects ('fatigue') are known to worsen performance as, for example, driving'. Boundary values for longitudinal (z-axis) and transverse (x- or y-axis) vibration are shown in figures 12.2 and 12.3 as a function of frequency and duration of exposure.

2 *The exposure limit.* This is deemed to be the maximum for 'the preservation of health and safety'. For all conditions it is set at *twice* the decreased proficiency boundary level. (The exposure limit is set at approximately half the threshold of pain for normal subjects.)

3 The *reduced comfort boundary.* This is set at a level defined by the reduced proficiency boundary *divided by 3.15.*

It is noted that where the rms acceleration exceeds 7 m/s² , then the peak acceleration is likely to be greater than g—hence people may be thrown up off their seats. This is unlikely to be a problem at frequencies greater than 20 Hz.

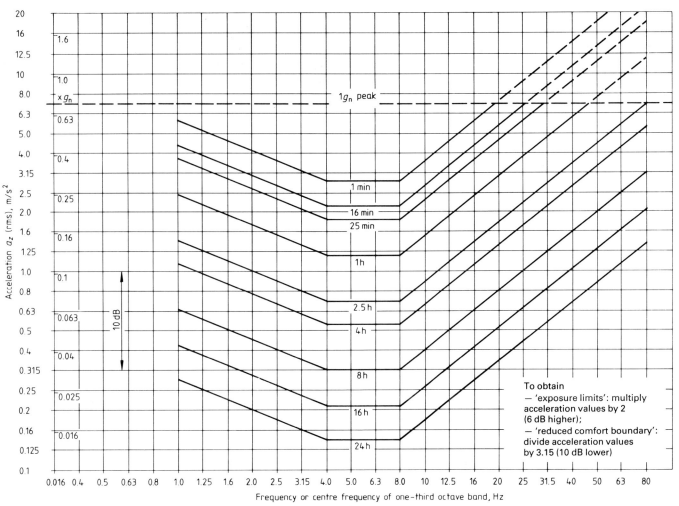

Figure 12.2 Longitudinal *(a$_z$)* **acceleration limits as a function of frequency and exposure time:** **'fatigue-decreased proficiency boundary'** From ISO 2631/1

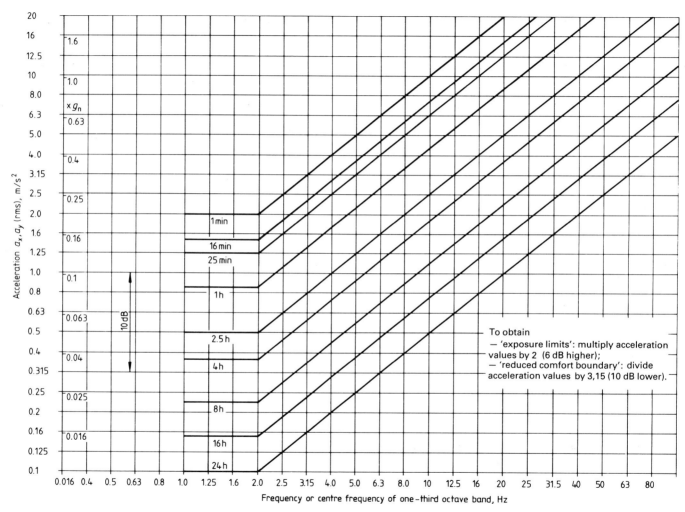

Figure 12.3 Transverse (a_x, a_y) **acceleration limits as a function of frequency and exposure time;** **'fatigue–decreased proficiency boundary'** From ISO 2631/1

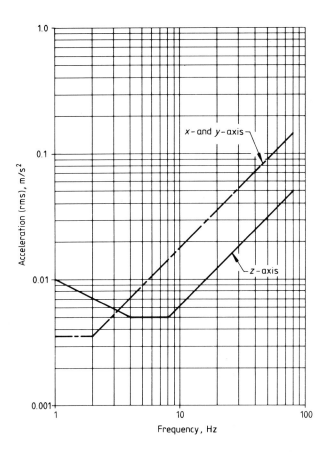

Figure 12.4 Building vibration *x*-, *y*- and *z*-axes base curve for acceleration (r.m.s)   Adapted from BS 6472

BS 6472 deals with the problem of structural vibration in buildings. It specifies 'base curves' which represent equal annoyance levels for frequencies of 1 Hz to 80 Hz (see figure 12.4). The frequency functions are in fact the same as those given in ISO 2631 although the levels are very much lower.

At vibration levels less than those specified in these curves 'adverse comments of vibration are rare'. The extent to which higher levels are likely to be acceptable depends upon circumstances. It is considered that for residential buildings two to four times the base level is acceptable by day or 1.4 times the base level by night; for offices four times the base level; for workshops eight times the base level.

Comment—Oborne (1981) has criticized ISO 2631 arguing that it is based on inadequate experimental evidence, particularly with respect to the extent to which acceptable levels are dependent upon duration of exposure.

12.2 Motion sickness

The symptoms of motion sickness, which are predominantly caused by vertical (z-axis) vibration of less than 0.63 Hz, progress from pallor and dizziness through nausea and vomiting to more or less complete prostration. Addendum 2 to ISO 2631 specifies a *severe discomfort boundary* within which some 90 % of men and 85 % of women might be expected to remain symptom-free (see figure 12.5). To provide a 90 % cover for women it is likely that accelerations would need to be reduced by around 20 %. (Values refer to inexperienced travellers who are most affected—however, about 5 % of people never adapt to motion at less than 0.63 Hz.) Children are more sensitive, elderly people less sensitive, and infants under 18 months more or less immune.

12.3 Hand/arm vibration

Hand-held power-tools commonly transmit vibration directly to the hand and arm. If excessive and prolonged this may lead to lesions of the bones and joints and/or a condition called *vibration white finger*, which is a neurovascular disorder leading to a painful and disabling blanching of the extremities, usually in the cold. Exposure limits for hand/arm vibration are at present extremely tentative. Figure 12.6 is taken from a BSI draft for development (DD 43) which is not to be regarded as a standard.

Additional information—Grandjean (1981, Ch 16), Oborne (1981, Ch 10), Singleton (1982, Ch 4).

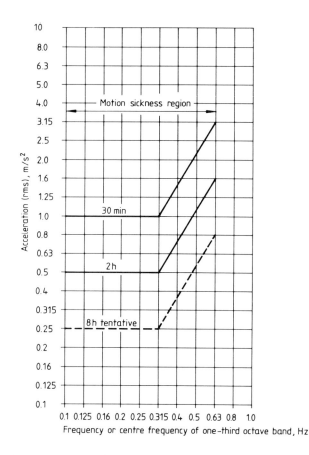

Note. These boundaries are subject to the qualifications in 3.1 in the complete standard.

**Figure 12.5 'Severe discomfort boundaries',
0.1 to 0.63 Hz for z-axis (a_z) vibration**
From ISO 2631/3

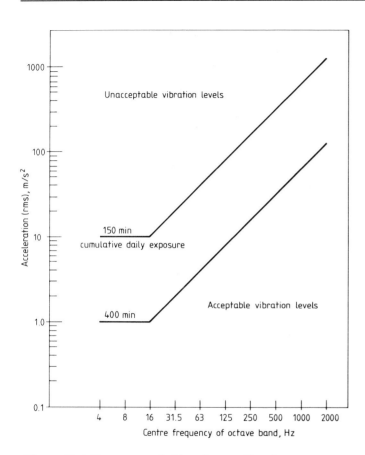

Figure 12.6 Recommended hand–arm vibration exposure limits for regular users   From DD 43

Section 13 Noise

Sound is a rapid oscillation of ambient air pressure (it may also be transmitted through other media). The audible range of frequencies extends from 20 Hz to 20 000 Hz (approximately 10 octaves). The exact limits vary between individuals—especially at the top end. Disturbances at higher frequencies than the audible range are called 'ultrasound'. Disturbances at lower frequencies, known as 'infra-sound' may, if sufficiently intense, be felt on the chest wall (as can sounds in the lower part of the audible range).

Noise is defined as sound which is undesired by the recipient. Any sound is a noise *if you do not wish to hear it*. The principal effects of noise—which by definition are all undesirable—are:
1. Hearing loss (which may be either temporary or permanent);
2. Interference with verbal communication;
3. Interference with the performance of mental work;
4. Annoyance.

13.1 Units

The energy level of a just detectable sound differs from that which ruptures the eardrum by a factor of around 10^{15}. It is convenient to measure the physical magnitude of sound on a logarithmic scale. The unit of this scale is the *decibel* (dB).

The *sound pressure level* (L_p) in decibels at any particular point (in space) is given by

$$L_p = 20 \log_{10} p/p_0$$

where p is the root mean square value of sound pressure at a particular point and p_0 is the reference level
$$(p_0 = 20\,\mu\text{Pa} = 2 \times 10^{-5}\ \text{N/m}^2).$$

The *sound power level* (L_w) in decibels emitted by a particular source is given by

$$L_w = 10 \log_{10} P/P_0$$

where P is the sound power of the source and P_0 is the reference level ($\approx 1\ \text{pW}$).

(See also BS 5775, BS 3045, etc.)

Note that an increase in sound level of 3 dB represents a doubling of the sound energy reaching the ear per unit time (since $\log_{10} 2 \approx 0.3$).

The *band pressure level* is the sound pressure level of the sound energy in a particular range of frequencies (for example, within a bandwidth of one octave).

Table 13.1 gives some examples of typical sound levels associated with various devices, activities and environments.

The human ear is not equally sensitive throughout its frequency range. Hence, the *subjective magnitude* or 'loudness' of a sound (as perceived or judged by a typical observer) is a function of both its *physical magnitude* and its frequency—this is the basis of the *phon* scale of *loudness level*. Furthermore the response of the human ear is non-linear with respect to sound intensity—this is the basis of the *sone* scale of *loudness*.

Loudness levels (phons), sound level (dB) and frequency (Hz) are related by a set figure of *equal loudness contours* as shown in figure 13.1 (adapted from BS 3383). The phon and decibel scales are numerically equal at a frequency of 1000 Hz. Hence a sound has a loudness level of *n* phons if it is judged to be of equal loudness as a 1000 Hz pure tone of *n* dB sound pressure level. The human ear is maximally sensitive in the 1000 Hz to 5000 Hz frequency range. The musical note 'high C' has a frequency of 1047 Hz—hence the piercing quality of trumpets and sopranos.

Table 13.1 Typical sound levels for various devices, activities or environments

Sound level

dB(A)

160	Blast from jet take-off, explosions, artillery fire, etc.
150	Rupture of ear drum
140	Shot gun (at ear)
	Threshold of pain
130	
120	Pneumatic hammer
	Chainsaw (at user)
110	Rock band (on stage or near speakers)
	Lawn mower (at user)
100	Jet flyover (1000 feet)
90	Motorcycle (7 metres)
	Personal stereo (inside ear canal)
80	Lathe
	Heavy traffic, noisy computer printer
70	Television
	Conversational speech at one metre
60	Noisy office (average level)
50	Typical office
40	'Quiet' office or residence
30	Quiet in the country, birdsong
20	Whisper at one metre
10	Soundproof room
0	Threshold of hearing

Note. Noise levels of devices are at the normal user or listener distance unless otherwise specified. Values are typical values and have been compiled from many sources.

It is expedient for many purposes for the frequency response of noise meters to approximate that of the human ear. This is the basis of the commonly used A-weighting scale. Sounds measured thus are designated by the symbol of dB(A). BS 5969 and BS 3539 deal with noise meters of various types.

13.2 Damage to hearing

Very intense noises (explosive blasts, etc.) may have an acute traumatic effect on the ear. These commence at about 130 dB(A) with the eardrum rupturing at 150 dB(A) or more. Less intense noise, down to about 80 dB(A), may cause hearing damage if exposure is prolonged. In the early stages, this is manifested as a temporary threshold shift (recovery from which is complete). Cumulative effects may lead to permanent hearing impairment. Risk of hearing damage is believed to be negligible at levels of 80 dB(A) or less.

ISO 1999 and BS 5330 both provide methods for estimating the risk of hearing damage as a result of occupational noise exposure. Risk is expressed as the estimated percentage of people whose hearing is impaired to the extent of a certain audiometric criterion.

(BS 5330 is based on a 30 dB elevation of audiometric threshold, whereas ISO 1999 is based on 25 dB—the frequencies at which audiometric thresholds are measured also differ.)

The methods of calculation are similar in principle but different in detail. Where noise level is steady throughout an 8-hour working day the associated risk may be determined directly. In other circumstances it is necessary to calculate a *continuous equivalent noise level*) (L_{eq}) which is derived from a tabulated function of sound level and duration of exposure (which differs very slightly in BS 5330 and ISO 1999). The tabulated function is (presumably) based on the principle of equal 'doses' of sound energy giving rise to equal levels of risk (although this principle is not stated

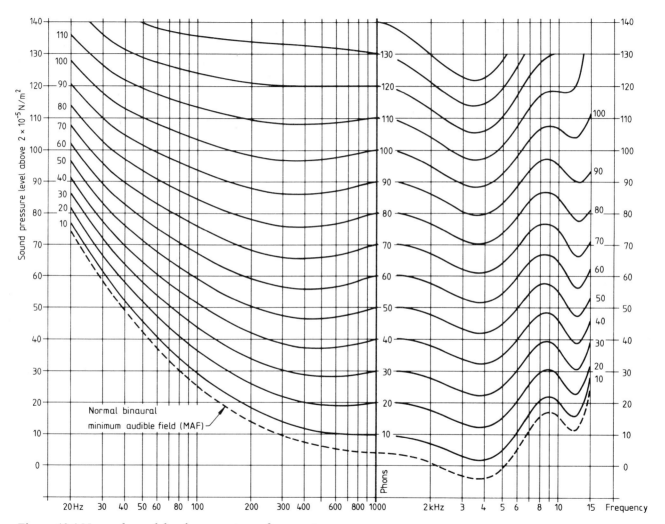

Figure 13.1 Normal equal-loudness contours for pure tones (Binaural free-field listening) Adapted from BS 3383

explicitly in either standard). Hence, exposure to a 90 dB(A) noise for eight hours per day gives rise to the same risk as 93 dB(A) for four hours, 96 dB(A) for two hours, etc.

Table 13.2 shows the risk of hearing impairment as a function of L_{eq} and years of exposure (on the assumption of a 4-hour week and 50 weeks per year) as presented in ISO 1999. For information, the case of $L_{eq} \leqslant 80$ dB(A) is included, the lower row (b) being the percentage of persons with impaired hearing in a non-noise-exposed group; this value is equal to the difference between corresponding table entries (b) and (a) for any noise-exposed group.

In the United Kingdom, the *recommended limits* for noise exposure at work are set out in a Health and Safety Executive code of practice (HSE 1978). This specifies a limit of 90 dB(A) for eight hours continuous exposure or equivalent sound level (L_{eq}) calculated on the equal energy principle. It also specifies an 'overriding condition' that the unprotected ear should not be exposed to a sound pressure level exceeding 135 dB or, in the case of impulse noise, an instantaneous sound pressure exceeding 150 dB.

In 1985, the European council of ministers issued a directive, concerning noise exposure at work, which sets a deadline of 1 January 1990 for the implementation of legislation in EEC countries. It refers to the daily personal noise exposure, which is identical to an 8-hour L_{eq}. When this level exceeds 85 dB(A), or the peak pressure exceeds 200 Pa, ear protectors and audiometric testing must be made available and the workforce must receive appropriate information and training. When the overall level exceeds 90 dB(A) or the peak pressure exceeds 200 Pa, the employer will be required to apply a programme of measures for reduction of noise exposure and the use of ear protectors will be compulsory.

HSE 1978 states that '. . . ear protectors should not be used as a substitute for effective noise control. They should normally be regarded as an interim measure while control of noise exposure by other means is being perfected'. In general, the purpose of protectors should be to reduce the sound levels *at the wearer's ear* to acceptable levels.

(In order to evaluate the efficiency of a particular ear protector in a particular situation it is necessary to establish the noise attenuations which it provides at different frequencies; to compare these with the octave band sound pressures of the noise; and to convert the results to a single A-weighted sound level.) BS 6344 deals with industrial hearing protectors (to date only Part 1 dealing with ear muffs has appeared). ISO 4869 describes a method for the measurement of the sound attenuation properties of hearing protectors.

Table 13.2 Risk of hearing impairment

a) Relation between equivalent continuous sound level during work in 0 to 45 years and risk of hearing impairment for conversational speech.

b) Total percentage of people with impaired hearing in a noise-exposed group. (Percentage of people with impaired hearing in a non-noise-exposed group is equal to percentage in a group exposed to continuous sound levels below 80 dB (A).)
(Years of exposure = Age − 18 years)

Equivalent continuous sound level db (A)		Risk, %, or Total % with impaired hearing	Percentages Years of exposure									
			0	5	10	15	20	25	30	35	40	45
≤ 80	a)	Risk, %	0	0	0	0	0	0	0	0	0	0
	b)	Total % with impaired hearing	1	2	3	5	7	10	14	21	33	50
85	a)	Risk, %	0	1	3	5	6	7	8	9	10	7
	b)	Total % with impaired hearing	1	3	6	10	13	17	22	30	43	57
90	a)	Risk, %	0	4	10	14	16	16	18	20	21	15
	b)	Total % with impaired hearing	1	6	13	19	23	26	32	41	54	65
95	a)	Risk, %	0	7	17	24	28	29	31	32	29	23
	b)	Total % with impaired hearing	1	9	20	29	35	39	45	53	62	73
100	a)	Risk, %	0	12	29	37	42	43	44	44	41	33
	b)	Total % with impaired hearing	1	14	32	42	49	53	58	65	74	83
105	a)	Risk, %	0	18	42	53	58	60	62	61	54	41
	b)	Total % with impaired hearing	1	20	45	58	65	70	76	82	87	91
110	a)	Risk, %	0	26	55	71	78	78	77	72	62	45
	b)	Total % with impaired hearing	1	28	58	76	85	88	91	93	95	95
115	a)	Risk, %	0	36	71	83	87	84	81	75	64	47
	b)	Total % with impaired hearing	1	38	74	88	94	94	95	96	97	97

Note — These values are based on the limited experimental data available at this time and are liable to revision when the results of further research become available.
From ISO 1999

13.3 Effects of noise on intelligibility of speech

The sounds of speech are within the 100 Hz to 8000 Hz range of frequencies, with most of the energy between 100 Hz and 600 Hz. Noise within this range produces *masking* and reduces the intelligibility of speech—defined as 'the ratio, expressed in per cent, of the number of sentences understood to the total number of sentences spoken during an ordinary conversation'. An intelligibility of not less than 95 % is deemed satisfactory (ISO/TR 3352). Table 13.3 shows the distances at which conversation is considered to be satisfactorily intelligible, as a function of a parameter of the ambient noise known as the *speech interference level* (defined as the arithmetic mean of the band pressure levels measured in the octave bands whose centre frequencies are 500 Hz, 1000 Hz, 2000 Hz and 4000 Hz).

13.4 Noise and performance

Noise may affect the performance of tasks by masking significant sound (auditory signals, clicking of switches, etc.). It may also adversely affect the psychological state of the operator in such a way as to make his performance (particularly of complicated tasks) erratic and predispose him to errors. In the industrial context it is more likely to affect the quality of work than the quantity. Steady noise is unlikely to affect performance at levels less than 90 dB(A); but irregular bursts of noise may have effects at lower levels.

Table 13.3 Maximum distances for the intelligibility of conversation in noisy environments

Speech interference level	Maximum distance at which normal conversation is considered to be satisfactorily intelligible	Maximum distance at which conversation in raised voice is considered to be satisfactorily intelligible
dB	m	m
35	7.5	15
40	4.2	8.4
45	2.3	4.6
50	1.3	2.6
55	0.75	1.5
60	0.42	0.85
65	0.25	0.50
70	0.13	0.26

From ISO/TR 3352

13.5 Annoyance

The most widespread effect of noise is the *annoyance* it causes.
(We might consider this a species of environmental *discomfort*.) This
can occur at relatively low sound levels, particularly if the noise
has information content (speech, music, etc.) or is taken as
evidence of someone else's inconsiderateness (motorcycles, parties,
sweet wrappers in the theatre). These effects do not lend
themselves to standardization but we might think of the following
as approximate maxima for auditory comfort:

Workshops	65 dB(A)
General office	55 dB(A)
Private office	40 dB(A)
Living room	30 dB(A)
Classroom or bedroom	25 dB(A)
Concert hall or theatre	20 dB(A)

Figures quoted from Bennett (1977)

BS 4142 deals with a method for rating industrial noise with respect
to the effects it might have on nearby residential areas. It is based
upon a 'comparison' between the noise level due to the industrial
process and the background noise level. When the former exceeds
the latter by more than 10 dB(A) complaints are considered likely.

Differences of 5 dB(A) are of marginal significance. If the noise
level due to the industrial process is more than 10 dB(A) below the
background level complaints are unlikely. It is necessary to correct
the industrial noise level, as initially measured, for various factors
such as the presence of identifiable tones or irregularities, the
intermittency and duration of the noise, and the time of day at
which it occurs. When the background level cannot be measured
directly, a notional value may be calculated based on the type of
factory, the type of neighbourhood, and the time of day.

Figure 13.2 is taken from an appendix to BS 4142 which deals with
frequency components of noise most likely to cause annoyance.
The oblique lines on the chart define zones of equal annoyance.
The octave bands of the industrial noise which protrude into the
highest zone are the ones most likely to cause annoyance.

Additional information—Various other British and International
standards deal with noise and its measurement. The reader is
referred to the relevant catalogues and handbooks for details.
Ergonomic aspects of noise are are covered in Grandjean (1981,
Ch 16), Oborne (1981, Ch 10) and Singleton (1982, Ch 7). Detailed
treatments of the effects of noise on human beings include Kryter
(1970) and Burns (1973).

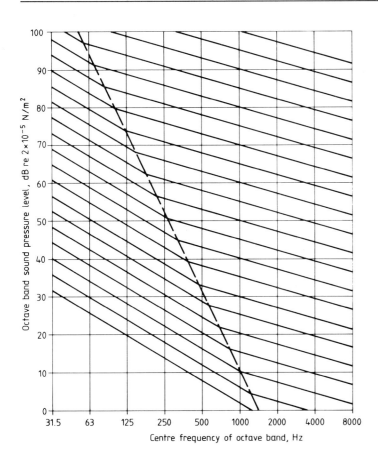

Figure 13.2 Chart to identify annoying component of noise
Adapted from BS 4142

Part Three
Information

The sections which follow are concerned with the presentation of information. Ergonomics books usually refer to any source of information, whether visual or otherwise, as a *display*. There is a minority of circumstances in which information should be communicated by an *auditory signal*—because it is necessary to get the user's attention (in order to indicate a hazard) or because his capacity to process visual information is fully occupied. But auditory signals are inherently intrusive and must be used with discretion if they are not to become irritants. In the vast majority of circumstances visual communication will be more appropriate—by means of media such as analogue and digital displays or the written word and its symbolic substitutes.

The information which is displayed should always be selected according to the tasks in which the user is engaged; and the information with the highest priority should be displayed most boldly. The failures in communication, which cause the greatest difficulty and frustration, usually result from the absence of a critical item of information or from the presence of irrelevant material, which the user must process before he finds what he requires—consider the signposts of a public building or the instruction manual of a complex product such as a computer.

If communication is to occur, the message must be seen; it must be read, recognized and distinguished from other messages; and it must be understood. In other words, the message must be *visible*, *legible*, and *intelligible*.

Section 14 Principles of display design

14.1 The mechanism of vision

The eye is a hollow, fluid-filled structure with a tough outer coating. It is approximately spherical in shape, and sits in a conical socket (the *orbit*) within which its position is controlled by six small muscles (hence allowing the optical axis of the eye to point in different directions).

Light enters the eye through its translucent front wall (the *cornea*), passes through an aperture (the *pupil*), and is focused by the *lens* on to the inner surface of the eye's back wall (the *retina*), which contains light-sensitive cells (the *rods* and *cones*) which transmit information to the brain. The diameter of the pupil is controlled by the muscles of the *iris* (the visible coloured part of the eye). The power of the lens is controlled by the *ciliary muscles*—these are relaxed when viewing a distant object (six metres to infinity) and increasingly tense as the object gets closer. This process is known as *accommodation*; it reaches its limit at the *near point* of vision which is around 120 mm from the eye in youth. The lens stiffens with age and we become more *long sighted*, finding it increasingly difficult to focus on close objects or to make rapid changes in focal distance. The near point typically reaches about 180 mm by 40 years of age and recedes rapidly thereafter, reaching about 250 mm at 45, 500 mm at 50 and 1000 mm at 60. This recession (*presbyopia*) becomes a problem when it is no longer possible to bring print into focus at a distance which is sufficiently close to read it. Spectacles are then required. The problem is exacerbated by the fact that *visual acuity* (the eye's capacity to resolve fine detail) also declines with age.

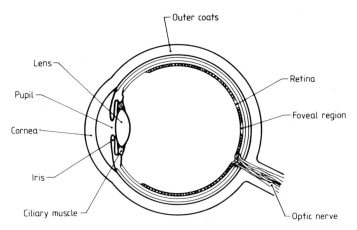

Figure 14.1 The eye

The two types of light-sensitive cells have different functions and are differently distributed about the retina. The rods are sensitive only to patterns of light and dark (particularly if these are moving) and are responsible for night (*scotopic*) vision; the cones are sensitive to differences in colour as well as to differences of light and dark, and also come into action under daylight conditions (*photopic* vision). The process of *dark adaptation* is discussed in section 10. The cones are most numerous in a small area, immediately surrounding the central visual axis of the eye, known as the *fovea*; the rods are found in peripheral parts of the retina.

Visual fields are usually described in terms of angles subtended at the eye. The centre of the visual field, equivalent to the optical axis of the eye, is known as the *line of sight*. The eye is only sufficiently sensitive to resolve the level of detail required, for tasks such as reading print or recognizing a face, in the central part of the visual field—within an area subtended by an angle of approximately two degrees around the line of sight. (At a reading distance of 400 mm this is equivalent to a circle of 14 mm radius around the central fixation point.) This region of *maximum acuity* is known as the area of *foveal vision*. In the immediately surrounding *parafoveal* area (2° to 10° from the axis, equivalent to a circle of 70 mm radius at a distance of 400 mm) acuity drops off rapidly and a person's capacity for the acquisition of visual information is correspondingly diminished. In the remaining *peripheral* part of the field we can only acquire vague impressions of light and shade—but we are quite sensitive to movements, 'glimpsed out of the corner of the eye'. Full colour vision is effectively limited to the foveal and parafoveal regions (and a little beyond in some directions).

We acquire information concerning our environment by the process of *visual search*, directing the line of sight first in one direction then another, so as to direct the 'spotlight' of foveal vision on different objects or features. Similarly, we read text by means of scanning movements (*saccades*) and relatively brief *fixations*. The length of a typical saccade is equivalent to around two degrees of visual angle (14 mm at 400 mm distance) with fixations lasting about ¼ second. (These figures will of course vary with the difficulty of the text, the skill of the reader, etc.)

14.2 Location of visual displays

Visual angle

In the relaxed position the eyes have a slight downward cast. This defines the *normal line of sight* which is held to be directed straight ahead (in the midline of the body) at an angle of 15° below the *horizontal line of sight* (drawn at eye level).

The preferred zone for the location of visual displays extends 15° in all directions from the normal line of sight. Hence, in the vertical plane it extends from the horizontal to an angle of 30° downwards. The gaze may be directed anywhere in this zone by eye movements

only. In plan view the preferred zone extends 15° either side of the mid-line. It is considered that a downward inclination of the head, of 15° or less, will not impose an excessive loading on the neck muscles (see section 6.1)—hence, the acceptable zone for the location of displays extends downwards, 15° beyond the preferred zone, to an angle of 45° below the horizontal.

Directing the gaze upwards is rapidly fatiguing; displays which are viewed for long periods of time should never be located above the horizontal line of sight. (This does not apply to public information notices, which are only viewed for short periods.)

Visual distance

The *maximum* distance for reading a display will be determined by factors related to its legibility and the subject's visual acuity. The closer a display to the subject's eyes, the greater the effort required for accommodation. If excessive, this may cause visual fatigue and 'eyestrain'. It is important therefore, that displays should be sufficiently bold (and well illuminated) to be read at a comfortable visual distance. People generally choose to read books, etc, at a visual distance of about 400 mm (± 50 mm). The minimum comfortable distance for reading instrumental displays (dials, VDUs, etc.) is considered to be 500 mm and 700 mm is probably preferable. Instruments for panel mounting are often designed to be read at an 'arm's length' distance of 710 mm (MIL-STD-1472C) or at 1000 mm (BS 3693).

14.3 Visibility

The *conspicuity* of an object (that is, the readiness with which it may be seen) increases with its size (i.e. the visual angle it subtends at the eye); its contrast and colour (see section 11.3); and its position in the visual field. In general, objects located within 15° of the line of sight will have the highest conspicuity. Note however, that an

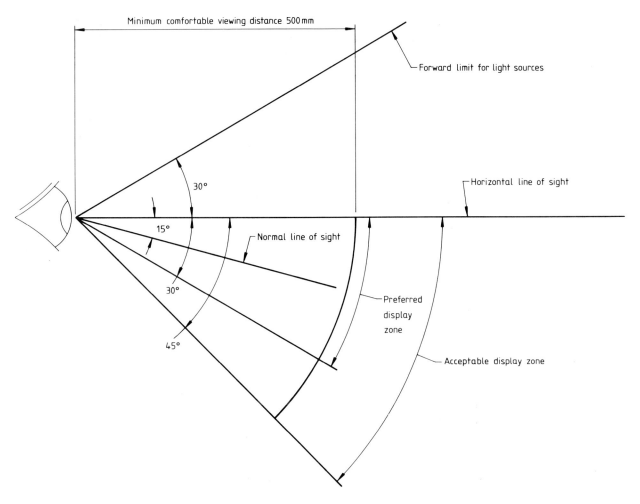

Figure 14.2 Preferred location for visual displays   From PP 7310

object which presents excessive contrast near the centre of the visual field is a potential source of glare (see section 10.2).

Legibility

In general, the legibility of text, symbols or any other displayed material *increases* with the following factors:

- Size
  Consider the ratio S/D where D is the viewing distance and S is the size of some feature or detail which is significant for the identification or reading of the display. This ratio determines the angle which the particular feature subtends at the eye: when S is small and D is large the ratio S/D is numerically equal to the angle in radians (rad). Given reasonable illumination and contrast, a person with 'normal' eyesight can resolve features which subtend an angle of one minute of arc. ($1' = \frac{1}{60}° = 0.0003$ rad). This is equivalent to a feature size of 0.3 mm for every metre of viewing distance.

- Contrast
  This commonly means low reflectance symbols on high reflectance ground (e.g. black on white) or vice versa (e.g. white on black). The former is preferred where ambient illumination is greater than 10 lux (MIL-STD-1472C). See also section 11.3 concerning colour contrast.

- Task illumination (see section 10.2)

- Absence of glare sources (see section 10.2)

- Simplicity of form
  In general, simple visual forms are easier to interpret than complex ones. Avoid visual clutter and visual 'noise'—'*less is more*'.

- Familiarity of message
  Familiar words, symbols, etc., are recognized more easily than novel ones.

- Duration of viewing

- Visual acuity of readers
  In general, acuity deteriorates with age, although this may be counteracted by wearing spectacles. However, as many as 40% of some adult populations may have uncorrected visual defects.

- The display surface should be, as nearly as possible, perpendicular to the line of sight. The effective size of a feature falls off with the cosine of the angle between the line of sight and the perpendicular to the display surface.

Note—To some extent the above factors may compensate for each other. Hence, we might move a page of text closer to our eyes (increase S/D) in order to compensate for poor light, smudgy print, etc.

Section 15 Typography

The following is concerned specifically with the *legibility* of printed alphanumeric material, including not only continuous text (such as books) but also labels, posters, etc.

Text which is difficult to read is necessarily difficult to understand—since the effort involved in visually distinguishing the words will distract the reader from the sense which they convey. (Perfectly legible text may of course be difficult to understand for other reasons which are discussed in section 18.)

15.1 Character size

The capital 'E' has five elements in the vertical plane—three strokes and two spaces. In principle therefore, it must subtend five minutes of visual arc (0.0015 rad) if it is to be just legible at the threshold of visual acuity. In practice larger letters are required. BS 3693 requires that the characters used for labels on instruments should subtend an angle of 16 minutes at the eye, which is equivalent to $0.0047D$, where D is the reading distance. A letter height of $0.005D$ is comfortably legible in most situations and $0.007D$ is generous.

Note—These recommendations are for the heights of *capital* letters and also *numerals*. Letter size may also be specified in terms of the *x-height*—that is, the height of a lower case letter, such as an 'x', which has neither an *ascender* nor a *descender* (see figure 15.1). The x-height may be anything between $0.6H$ and $0.8H$ (where H is the capital height) depending on the typeface.

The point system

Regrettably, the archaic *point* system, for the specification of type size, is still widely used. There are two different versions.

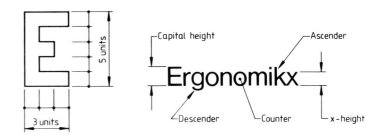

Figure 15.1 Terms for letter heights

One Anglo-American point (pt) is approximately ¹⁄₇₂ inch. (To be precise, 1 Anglo-American pt = 0.0138 in = 0.351 mm.) In much of Europe however, the Didot point is used: 1 Didot pt = 0.376 mm = 1.07 Anglo-American pt.

The point size is the body size of the metal type used in printing, extending from somewhere above the tops of the capitals to somewhere below the descenders. It does not correspond to any visible characteristics of the actual characters on the printed page. (In the case of phototypeset letters, the point size is a measure of what the body height would have been had metal type been used.) Considerable differences exist between typefaces. Hence, 10 pt letters in one face may have the same character size on the printed page as 12 pt letters in another; and 10 pt letters in different typefaces may have capitals ranging from less than 2 mm to almost 3 mm in height. Attempts to bring order to this chaos have not yet proved successful.

15.2 The shape and style of letters

Under normal viewing conditions a wide range of commonly used (and some less common) typefaces are more or less equally legible. Excessively ornamented faces, or features such as hairline strokes, extended serifs, or shadow effects cause difficulties if viewing conditions are poor or if the message must be read quickly. Restraint is generally called for. Recommendations may be summarized as follows:

- Capitals such as 'B', 'E', 'F' have five elements in the vertical plane and three in the horizontal (see figure 15.1). If each subtends an equal visual angle then the width will be $0.6H$ (height). This is recommended in MIL-STD 1472C (except for 'M' and 'W' which should be $0.8H$ and 'I' which should be one stroke wide).

- Empirical studies summarized by McCormick and Saunders (1982) show that a character width of $0.7H$ to $0.85H$ is optimal and that the width of each individual stroke should be $0.125H$ to $0.133H$ for black on white, or $0.1H$ to $0.125H$ for white on black.

- Lower case letters should have large open *counters*.

- Roman letters of medium weight are generally easier to read than their italic, light, bold, condensed or expanded variants.

- In almost all applications (ranging from continuous text to road signs) mixed capitals and lower case are easier to read than capitals used alone. However, for the labels on instruments, etc. capitals alone are commonly recommended (MIL-STD 1427C for example). When vertical space is severely limited capitals may permit it to be used more efficiently (this can result in an increase in letter size of about 20%, which may give greater legibility). However, text set in capitals occupies a horizontal space (i.e. line length) which is about 40% greater than mixed characters of equivalent size.

- It is widely considered that for *continuous text* serif faces (Times Roman, Baskerville, Plantin, etc.) are 'easier on the eye'. The serifs are said to increase the distinguishing features for individual letters (particularly the top halves which are

important for character recognition) and to help join them up into meaningful groups. It may well be that this supposed superiority is largely a matter of tradition and familiarity.

For *isolated words such as labels* and for *relatively short messages*, sans-serif faces are more legible. (Helvetica, Univers, Gill Sans, Futura, etc. are all excellent.)

15.3 Spacing

The *average spacing between letters* should be around $1 \pm \frac{1}{2}$ stroke width (or $0.13H$). Ideally this should be modified according to the shapes of the characters concerned.

The *average space between words* should be around three stroke widths (or $0.5H$). When using metal type this is equivalent to the width of a lower case 'i'.

The *space between lines* should be $1.5H$ to $1.6H$. That is, there should be a $0.5H$ to $0.6H$ gap between the base of one line and the top of the capitals of the next. This is equivalent to a 1 pt or 2 pt 'leading' on 8 pt to 10 pt type. *Justified text* (in which the right hand margin is aligned as well as the left) may result in excessively uneven word spacing which can increase the difficulty of reading (especially with short line lengths).

15.4 Page size

Although large page sizes give the designer greater flexibility of layout they lead to a finished product which is unwieldy in use. This may adversely affect legibility, since large pages will commonly be held at an oblique angle to the line of sight.

Table 15.1 ISO-A and ISO-B series of trimmed paper sizes

A – Series		B – Series	
Designation	Size mm	Designation	Size mm
		B0	1000 × 1414
A0	841 × 1189	B1	707 × 1000
A1	594 × 841	B2	500 × 707
A2	420 × 594	B3	353 × 500
A3	297 × 420	B4	250 × 353
A4	210 × 297	B5	176 × 250
A5	148 × 210	B6	125 × 176
A6	105 × 148	B7	88 × 125
A7	74 × 105	B8	62 × 88
A8	52 × 74	B9	44 × 62
A9	37 × 52	B10	31 × 44
A10	26 × 37		

From BS 4000, ISO 216 and others

Standard paper sizes (as specified in BS 4000, ISO 216 and others) have the proportions $\sqrt{2}:1 = 1.414:1$ (see figure 15.2). This means that they may be divided in half, parallel to the short edge, to give two sheets which have the same proportions as the original (see figure 15.3). The ISO-A (main) and ISO-B (supplementary) series of trimmed paper sizes are shown in table 15.1. A0 has an area of 1 m²: B0 has an area of $\sqrt{2}$m².

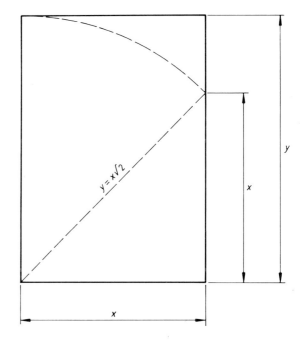

Figure 15.2 Illustration that the ratio between sides equals the ratio between the side and the diagonal of a square From BS 4000

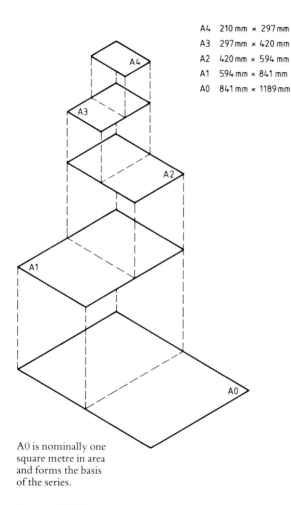

A4	210 mm × 297 mm
A3	297 mm × 420 mm
A2	420 mm × 594 mm
A1	594 mm × 841 mm
A0	841 mm × 1189 mm

A0 is nominally one
square metre in area
and forms the basis
of the series.

Figure 15.3 Relationship of the 'A' sizes

An alternative system of standard sizes for hardback (case-bound) books is described in BS 1413. Trimmed page sizes from this system (which also includes A4 and A5) are given in table 15.2.

Table 15.2 Page sizes for hardback books

	Octavo	Quarto
	mm	mm
Metric crown	186 × 123	246 × 189
Metric large crown	198 × 129	258 × 201
Metric demy	216 × 138	276 × 219
Metric royal	234 × 156	312 × 237

From BS 1413

15.5 Layout

The average length of a word in the English language is approximately five letters. For *continuous text* the optimum *line length* is considered to be 10 to 12 words or 60 to 70 characters (including spaces). In the advertising industry, a line length of seven words (or 42 characters) is considered optimal for captions, slogans, etc.

If all else is equal, single column formats are preferable to double. On A4 size however, the use of single columns will lead to excessive line lengths or needlessly large margins. In most cases a double column layout will be an acceptable solution. For certain kinds of material, the additional flexibility it gives will be an advantage.

The present book has been designed and written according to the ergonomic guidelines given in this section and in section 18. The page size is B5, used in landscape. This was chosen to combine maximum flexibility of layout with minimum overall dimensions.

It was considered that A4 would have been too bulky for convenient use (at the drawing board etc.); and that A5 would have excessively constrained the layout of text and figures. The choice of a size from the non-preferred B series was therefore considered to be justified (in spite of the fact that printing on A4 is cheaper.) The typeface is 11 point Bembo on a 12 point line spacing to give slightly greater legibility. The text is not justified and paragraphs are indicated by additional spacing rather than an indention. The two column layout gives a maximum line length of 70 characters. The sectional headings are 18 point Bembo bold; the numbered sub-sections 12 point Bembo bold; and other subheadings are 12 point Bembo.

Additional information—Extensive treatments of the legibility of print and related issues include Tinker (1963), Spencer (1969) and Hartley (1978). Easterby and Zwaga (1984) is an extensive collection of papers on the subject of information design.

15.6 Lettering on technical drawings

ISO 3098 Part 1 deals with the stencilled or free-hand lettering used on technical drawings. It specifies standard heights of 2.5, 3.5, 5, 7, 10, 14 and 20 mm. The lettering may be vertical or inclined 15° to the right. Two sets of specifications are given having a ratio of stroke width to letter height (w/h) of $\frac{1}{14}$ and $\frac{1}{10}$ respectively (see table 15.3).

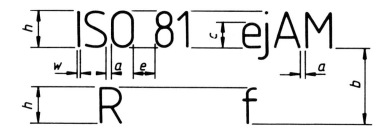

Table 15.3 Lettering

Characteristic		Ratio	Dimensions (mm)						
A) ($w = h/14$)									
Lettering height									
Height of capitals	h	$(14/14)\,h$	2.5	3.5	5	7	10	14	20
Height of lower-case letters (without stem or tail)	c	$(10/14)\,h$	—	2.5	3.5	5	7	10	14
Spacing between characters	a	$(2/14)\,h$	0.35	0.5	0.7	1	1.4	2	2.8
Minimum spacing of base lines	b	$(20/14)\,h$	3.5	5	7	10	14	20	28
Minimum spacing between words	e	$(6/14)\,h$	1.05	1.5	2.1	3	4.2	6	8.4
Thickness of lines	w	$(1/14)\,h$	0.18	0.25	0.35	0.5	0.7	1	1.4
B) ($w = h/10$)									
Lettering height									
Height of capitals	h	$(10/10)\,h$	2.5	3.5	5	7	10	14	20
Height of lower-case letters (without stem or tail)	c	$(7/10)\,h$	—	2.5	3.5	5	7	10	14
Spacing between characters	a	$(2/10)\,h$	0.5	0.7	1	1.4	2	2.8	4
Minimum spacing of base lines	b	$(14/10)\,h$	3.5	5	7	10	14	20	28
Minimum spacing between words	e	$(6/10)\,h$	1.5	2.1	3	4.2	6	8.4	12
Thickness of lines	w	$(1/10)\,h$	0.25	0.35	0.5	0.7	1	1.4	2

Note. The spacing a between two characters may be reduced by half if this gives a better visual effect, as for example LA, TV; it then equals the line thickness w.
From ISO 3098/1

Section 16 Symbols

Graphic symbols are used to transmit messages independently of written language. The object or concept which a symbol 'stands for' is known as its *referent*. Symbols may be abstract or representational. If representational they are sometimes known as *pictograms*.

The advantage of symbols and pictograms over written language is that they do not require either literacy or a knowledge of the language concerned. Their disadvantage is that they lack the precision of words—especially for conveying complex information. Symbols, especially pictographic ones, may be used to convey hazard warnings, etc. in a direct and immediate fashion. Compare the skull and cross-bones sign in table 16.3 with its verbal equivalent.

In general, symbols and pictograms are effective for identifying objects, pointing to their locations or describing their salient characteristics. They tend to be ineffective for giving any but the simplest of instructions. The more familiar a symbol the more effective it becomes.

The meaning of a symbol should be explicit, unambiguous and, as far as possible, self-evident. Questions of symbol design may be divided into those concerning what to show (*content*) and those concerning how to show it (*form*). It is rarely possible to provide explicit guidelines concerning content—the images which will most effectively suggest a particular referent will generally be context specific.

Given that content is appropriate, the principal characteristic of an effective symbol is economy of visual form. The symbol should be perceived as a meaningful whole (a *Gestalt*) rather than a collection of unrelated parts. The specific recommendations given below are all subordinate to this basic principle.

ISO 3461 deals with graphic symbols in general—including those intended for use in public places, on products and equipment, or on plans, diagrams and other documents. It includes the 'basic pattern' or grid, shown in figure 16.1a, which consists of eight geometrically related figures (three squares, two circles, two rectangles and a regular octagon). Figure 16.1b shows examples of the application of this grid in the design of symbols. The standard recommends that symbols should be drawn on the basic grid (at the scale shown in figure 16.1a) in lines of 2 mm width or 4 mm width if the situation demands; that the minimum spacing between lines should

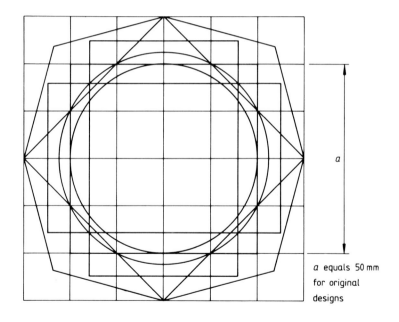

a

a equals 50 mm
for original
designs

Figure 16.1a Basic pattern or grid for the design of symbols
From ISO 3461

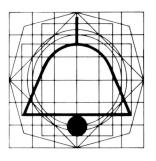
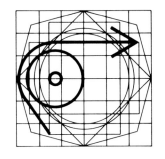
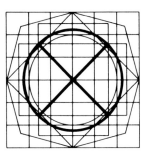
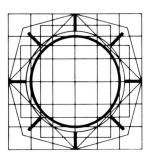

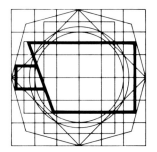
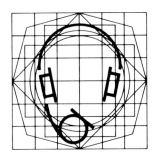

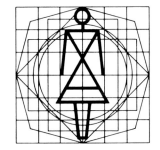

Figure 16.1b Examples of application   From ISO 3461

be 1.5 times the minimum line width; that angles smaller than 30° should be avoided; and that filled areas should be avoided as much as possible.

ISO 7001 deals specifically with public information symbols. It is supplemented by a technical report (ISO/TR 7239) which discusses the basic principles underlying the design and development of an effective symbol and includes a set of design criteria which could be held to represent the state of the art.

ISO/TR 7239 departs from the current (1976) version of ISO 3461 in two particular respects. First, it proposes that 'grids may help to maintain similar apparent size and consistency within sets of symbols' but warns that 'no symbol design should be forced to fit within a basic grid to the detriment of its communication'. Second, it recommends silhouette (filled) forms rather than outlines. It is possible that the content of ISO/TR 7239 might be incorporated into future versions of ISO 3461. ISO/TR 7239 includes the following design recommendations for public information symbols:

- Only those details which contribute to a better comprehension of the symbol should be included.

- Silhouette is preferable to outline. If outline is required, then the interior of the symbol should differ from the background in colour or pattern.

- Symbols with left/right symmetry are preferable to asymmetrical symbols.

- The design of symbols which convey directional information should permit reversal; conflicts with directional arrows should be avoided.

- Symbols which are similar in height and width are preferable to long narrow shapes (ratio of height and width should not exceed 4:1).

- The size of significant details (m) should be at least 1 mm for every metre of viewing distance (D): see figure 16.2. Hence, $m \geqslant 0.001D$. This represents a safety factor of three over the theoretical minimum of one minute of arc (as discussed in section 14.3).

- Where there is no interference from other visual elements, line width of significant details (w) should not be less than 0.5 mm for each metre of viewing distance. Hence, $w \geqslant 0.0005D$. (Safety factor of 1.5.)

- Symbols should generally be presented within square enclosures as shown in figure 16.2. (Diamond, circular or triangular enclosures may be used in some circumstances.) The distance between the edge of the symbol and the inner edge of the enclosures should exceed $1.5m$ or $2.5m$ if the edges are parallel. (Corners of enclosures may be rounded.)

- Symbol size (Z) will generally be specified as the length of the internal edge of the square enclosure.

It is recommended that for legibility (where conspicuity is not a concern) $Z = 0.012D$; for legibility and conspicuity $Z = 0.025D$. (These sizes are based on the assumption that the symbol will be located within 15° of the user's line of sight.)

For general purposes, symbols should not be displaced by more than 15° from the line of sight. Critical symbols should not be

Figure 16.2a Example of significant detail
From ISO/TR 7239

Figure 16.2b Example of line width for significant detail
From ISO/TR 7239

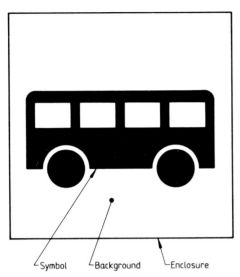

Figure 16.2c Structural elements of a sign
— Symbol   — Background   — Enclosure

Figure 16.2c Structural elements of a sign
From ISO/TR 7239

displaced by more than 5°. Where the symbol is below eye level, and may consequently be obscured, it may be necessary to increase its size. Symbols should not be placed at more than 5° below eye level. (5° is equivalent to a displacement of $0.12D$ from the line of sight; 15° is equivalent to a displacement of $0.25D$.)

(From ISO/TR 7239)

The public information symbols of ISO 7001 have been standardized in terms of a verbal description of image content; the function or referent of the symbol; and the intended area of application. (It is argued that the widely differing circumstances in which symbols are used preclude more rigid recommendations.) These are followed by a set of 'guideline examples' as shown in table 16.1.

Elsewhere, a more direct approach to the standardization of

symbols has been taken. ISO 7000 is a catalogue of symbols for use on products of various sorts—motor vehicles, office machines, industrial equipment, etc.

BS 5378 is a detailed specification for a system of safety colours and safety signs for conveying messages related to health and safety, that is, for the prevention of accidents, for warning people of health hazards or the necessity of wearing protective clothing, etc. The colours red, yellow, blue and green have defined meanings as shown in table 16.2.

The colorimetric properties of these colours are defined in Part 2 of the standard—see section 11.2. Examples of the various standardized types of safety signs are given in table 16.3. A range of other symbols is presented in tables 16.4 to 16.9. For a complete list of graphical symbols refer to the BSI Catalogue or, for an introduction, PP 7307.

Additional information—Easterby and Zwaga (1984) contains papers concerning symbol design. Graphical symbols for use on drawings in mechanical and electrical engineering, data processing, etc., are not our concern here. For an introduction refer to PP 7307.

Table 16.1 Public information symbols
Standard image content

No.	Name of symbol	Standard image content	Function
1	Male, man	Male figure	To signify a facility reserved for the male sex
2	Female	Female figure	To signify a facility reserved for the female sex
3	Drinking water (on tap)	Tap above glass containing water indicated by wavy lines	To signify drinkable tap water
4	Stairs	a) Where no direction is required: staircase with two human figures, one walking up, one walking down b) For staircases restricted to 'down' traffic: staircase with one figure walking down c) For staircases restricted to 'up' traffic: staircase with one figure walking up	To signify access facilities via a fixed staircase (does not cover the function 'Escalator')
5	Waiting room	Two persons in side view with a clock overhead	To signify where people may wait, in stations or hospitals
6	Telephone	Telephone receiver in profile	To signify communication facilities by telephone
7	Gasoline station	Gasoline pump with hose	To signify the availability of motor fuel
8	Direction	Arrow with Belgian head, with angle at apex of between 84° and 86°	To indicate direction
9	Taxi	Front view of taxi cab with 'TAXI' incorporated into the symbol Note. For small-scale reproduction, the word 'TAXI' may be omitted.	To signify a transport facility by taxi
10	Bus	Bus in side view	To signify a transport facility by bus
11	Tram (streetcar)	Electric tram (streetcar) in side view	To signify a transport facility by tram
12	Helicopter	Helicopter in side view	To signify a transport facility by helicopter
13	Smoking allowed	Cigarette with smoke in side view	To signify where smoking is allowed

Guide-line examples of public information symbols

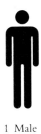

1 Male

2 Female

3 Drinking water (on tap)

4 Stairs

5 Waiting room

6 Telephone

7 Petrol station

8 Direction

9 Taxi

10 Bus

Telephone

Petrol station

Guide-line examples simplified for small–scale reproduction

11 Tram (streetcar)

12 Helicopter

13 Smoking allowed

From ISO 7001

Table 16.2 Safety signs: colours and layout

Sign	Meaning or purpose	Examples of use	Layout
	Stop	Stop signs Identification and colour of emergency shutdown devices Prohibition signs	Background colour shall be white. Circular band and cross bar shall be red. The symbol shall be black and placed centrally on the background, and shall not obliterate the cross bar. Red shall cover at least 35% of the area of the safety sign. Note. Any text is to be put on a supplementary sign.
	Caution, risk of danger	Indication of hazards (fire, explosion, radiation, chemical, etc.) Warning signs Identification of thresholds, dangerous passages, obstacles	Background colour shall be yellow. Triangular band shall be black. The symbol or text shall be black and placed centrally on the background. Yellow shall cover at least 50% of the area of the safety sign.
	Mandatory action	Obligation to wear personal safety equipment Mandatory signs	Background colour shall be blue. The symbol or text shall be white and placed centrally on the background. Blue shall cover at least 50% of the area of the safety sign.
	Safe condition	Identification of safety showers, first-aid posts and rescue points Emergency exit signs	Background colour shall be green. The symbol or text shall be white. The shape of the sign shall be oblong or square as necessary to accommodate the symbol or text. Green shall cover at least 50% of the area of the safety sign.
	Danger identification	Used to identify the perimeter of a hazard	Stripes are fluorescent orange-red or yellow and black in either case.

From BS 5378

Table 16.3 Examples of safety signs: prohibition, mandatory and warning

 No smoking

 Eye protection must be worn

 Caution, risk of fire

 Caution, overhead load

 Smoking and naked flames prohibited

 Head protection must be worn

 Caution, risk of explosion

 Caution, industrial trucks

 Pedestrians prohibited

 Hearing protection must be worn

 Caution toxic

 Caution, risk of electric shock

 Do not extinguish with water

 Respiratory protection must be worn

 Caution, corrosive substance

General warning, caution, risk of danger

 Not drinking water

 Foot protection must be worn

 Caution, risk of ionizing radiation

 Caution, laser beam

 Do not use ladder

 Hand protection must be worn

 Caution slippery surface

 Caution, guard dog(s)

Table 16.4 Fire safety signs

A warning sign

A mandatory sign

A prohibition sign

Straight on from here

or

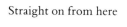

A fire equipment sign

Safe condition signs

Left from here

Right from here

Symbol alone

Highly flammable material

Highly flammable material

Wording and symbol

Up and left from here

Up and right from here

Down and left from here

Down and right from here

From BS 5499: Part 1

Table 16.5 Symbols for controls, indicators or tell-tales for road vehicles

Upper beam

Seat belt

Horn

Engine oil

Rear window
demisting and
defrosting

Windshield wiper
(may be combined
with symbol below)

Rear hood (boot)

Lower beam

Ventilating fan

Fuel

Lighter

Neutral indicator
(on motorcycles)

Windshield washer

Choke
(cold starting aid)

Turn signals

Parking lights

Engine coolant
temperature

Front fog light

Electric starter
(on motorcycles)

Master lighting
switch

Off
(on motorcycles)

Hazard warning

Front hood
(bonnet)

Battery charging
condition

Rear fog light

Run
(on motorcycles)

Windscreen
demisting and
defrosting

Engine ignition
cut-off
(on mopeds)

From BS AU 143c, ISO 6727, ISO 4129

Table 16.6 Symbol for machine tools

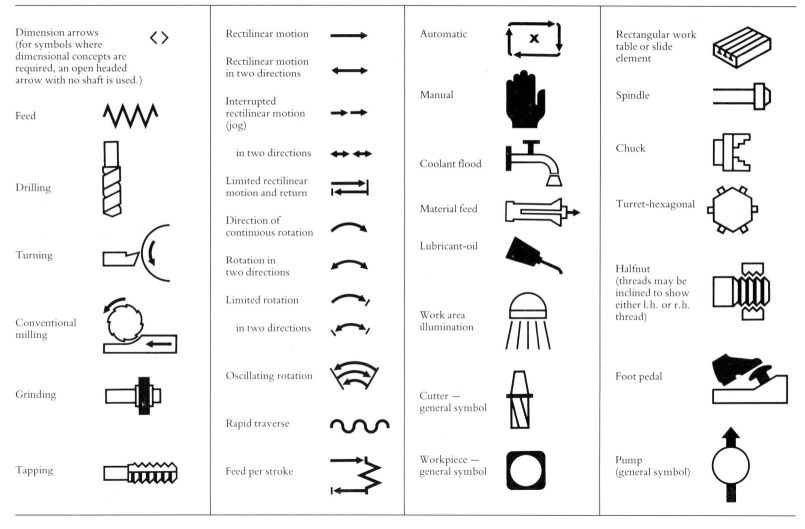

Dimension arrows (for symbols where dimensional concepts are required, an open headed arrow with no shaft is used.)

Feed

Drilling

Turning

Conventional milling

Grinding

Tapping

Rectilinear motion

Rectilinear motion in two directions

Interrupted rectilinear motion (jog)

   in two directions

Limited rectilinear motion and return

Direction of continuous rotation

Rotation in two directions

Limited rotation

   in two directions

Oscillating rotation

Rapid traverse

Feed per stroke

Automatic

Manual

Coolant flood

Material feed

Lubricant-oil

Work area illumination

Cutter — general symbol

Workpiece — general symbol

Rectangular work table or slide element

Spindle

Chuck

Turret-hexagonal

Halfnut (threads may be inclined to show either l.h. or r.h. thread)

Foot pedal

Pump (general symbol)

Table 16.6 (continued)

Revolution

Time-seconds
(for minutes replace
s with min and for
hours, h)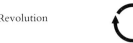

Weight
(the measured quantity
and units may be
superimposed)

Temperature
(may be used to
indicate:
    high temperature
    low temperature)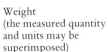

Increase of value
    e.g. speed,
    depth of cut

Decrease of value

Stepless regulation

Adjustable
(can be superimposed
on associated
symbols)

Lock or tighten

Unlock or untighten

Stop/off

Start/on

Start and stop with
same control

In action as long as
control operated
Ring-shaped symbol
in red, vertical bar
and 'T' in green

Emergency stop
Large convex button
entirely red

Engage

Disengage

Direction of
spindle rotation

Number of
revolutions per
minute (spindle
speed)

Feed per
revolution

Feed per minute

x is the value
of the feed to appear
either before the symbol
or in the corresponding
numerical table

Speed of
turning cut

Peripheral speed
of drill
x is the number
of revolutions to
appear either
before the symbol
or on the
corresponding
numerical table
xmm/min

Load work

Unload work

Coolant pump

Examples of
grouping
of symbols

Presentations and
withdrawal of
tapping spindle
with respect to
workpiece
(Where it is not
possible to define
exactly the
direction in
space it is often
useful to define
relative motion
between two
machine parts;
truncated arrow
heads are used
in pairs.)

Plate adjacent to a
lever showing the
feed in either
direction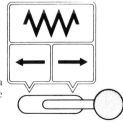

From BS 3641: Part 1

Table 16.7 Symbols for use on electrical equipment

Positioning
of cell

Stand-by

Foot switch

Treble control

Television
receiver

Stereophonic

AC/DC convertor,
rectifier, substitute
power supply

On/off
(push-button)

Lamp; lighting;
illumination

Bell

Colour television
Monitor

Balance

On (power)

On/off
(push-push)

Music

Tuner
Radio receiver

Colour
television camera

Colour

(qualifying symbol; when
the symbol is reproduced
multi-coloured, the
colours red, blue and
green should be shown in
the sequence left,
top, right)

Off (power)

Variability

Bass control

Tuning

Monophonic

From BS 6217

Table 16.7 (continued)

Contrast	Hue	Input	Play-back or reading from tape	Monitoring during play-back or reading from tape	Pause; interruption
Focus	Horizontal picture shift	Output	Erasing from tape	Normal run	Video tape recorder
Brightness; brilliance	Vertical picture shift	Stereophonic pick-up for disc records	Monitoring at the input during recording on tape	Fast run	Video recording
Colour saturation	Movement in both directions	Recording on tape	Monitoring from tape after recording on tape	Stop (of action)	Rejection

From BS 6217

Table 16.8 Textile care labelling

 machine wash at 60 °C, normal mechanical action

 machine wash at 40 °C, reduced mechanical action

 machine wash at 40 °C, much reduced mechanical action

 hand wash

 do not bleach

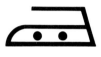 may be ironed with a warm iron

 may be ironed with a hot iron

may be tumble dried

 Articles which are safe to dry clean in all solvents normally used for dry cleaning (the letter inside the circle may be A, P or F depending on the solvents that can be used). The bar may also appear beneath the dry cleaning symbol to indicate restrictions concerning mechanical action and/or drying temperature

From BS 2747

Table 16.9 Pictorial marking of goods in transit

 Fragile Handle with care

 Keep dry

 Centre of gravity

 Sling here

 Use no hooks

 This way up

 Keep away from heat

 Protect from heat and radioactive sources

From ISO 780

Section 17 Display instruments

Product or panel mounted instruments may be divided into three main categories:

1 *Qualitative* displays such as warning lights, on/off indicators;
2 *Digital* displays, which give quantitative information in numerical form;
3 *Analogue* displays in which a pointer or *index* moves around a scale (or vice versa) in order to indicate the value of some quantity.

VDUs may be used in any of these modes.

17.1 Qualitative displays

BS 4099 deals with indicator lights, push buttons, annunciators and digital readouts. Part 1 of this standard is identical with IEC 73. Indicator lights are used to give the operator information concerning the state or condition of his equipment. Lights may be incorporated into push buttons to command the operator or to give direct feedback of activation. (Illuminated push buttons should never be used as emergency-stop buttons since the failure of a lamp could lead to erroneous conclusions.) An annunciator is a device that displays an illuminated message or legend. If the message is variable, that is, if it is selected from a set of characters by means of coded signals, the display is referred to as a digital readout.

For general purposes, a steady light will be used for indicators and for illuminated push buttons. Flashing lights may be employed for special purposes, where emphasis is required:

- to attract further attention;
- to request immediate action;
- to indicate a discrepancy between the required state and the actual state of the equipment;
- to indicate change in progress (flashing during the transition period).

Frequency of flashing may be used to indicate priority.

Standard practice in the selection of colours for indicator lights and push buttons is shown in tables 17.1 and 17.2 (from IEC 73).

Two flashing rates, $f1$ and $f2$, are recognized in IEC 73. The highest rate shall be used to indicate information with the highest priority. The permitted ranges for flashing frequencies are:
— $f1$: slow flashing, 0.4 Hz to 0.8 Hz (24 to 48 flashes per minute)
— $f2$: normal flashing, 1.4 Hz to 2.8 Hz (84 to 168 flashes per minute)

When only one rate is used it shall be $f2$. When two rates are used the ratio of $f1$:$f2$ shall be at least 1:2.5 and not more than 1:5. A ratio of 1:4 is recommended (for example 0.5 Hz and 2 Hz). The ON (or PULSE) time of the light should be about equal to the OFF (or PAUSE) time.

For $f1$ the PULSE may be longer than the PAUSE; for $f2$ the PAUSE may be longer than the PULSE; but in neither case should the ratio of lengths exceed 2:1.

Table 17.3 summarizes the recommended uses of flashing light as given in BS 4099:Part 2. Rapid flashing denotes $f2$ and slow flashing $f1$, as given in IEC 73.

Table 17.1 Colours of indicator lights and their meanings

Colour	Meaning	Explanation	Typical applications
Red	Danger or alarm	Warning of potential danger or a situation which requires immediate action	— Failure of pressure in lubricating system — Temperature outside specified (safe) limits — Essential equipment stopped by action of a protective device — Danger from accessible live or moving parts
Yellow	Caution	Change or impending change of conditions	— Temperature (or pressure) different from normal level — Overload, the duration of which is permitted for limited time only
Green	Safety	Indication of a safe situation or authorization to proceed, clear way	— Cooling liquid circulating — Automatic boiler control in operation — Machine ready to be started
Blue	Specific meaning assigned according to the need in the case considered	Blue may be given any specific meaning which is *not* covered by the three above colours: red, yellow and green	— Indication or remote control — Selector switch in "set up" position
White	No specific meaning assigned (neutral)	Any meaning, may be used whenever doubt exists about the application of the three colours red, yellow and green and, for example, for confirmation	

From IEC 73

Table 17.2 Colours of push buttons and their meaning

Colour	Meaning of colour	Typical applications
Red	Action in case of emergency STOP or OFF	— Emergency stop — Fire-fighting — General stop — To stop one or more motors — To stop a part of a machine — To open a switching device — Reset combined with STOP
Yellow	Intervention	Intervention to suppress abnormal conditions or to avoid unwanted changes
Green	START or ON	— General start — To start one or more motors — To start a part of a machine — To close a switching device
Blue	Any specific meaning not covered by the above colours	A meaning not covered by the colours red, yellow and green can be allocated to this colour in particular cases
Black Grey White	No specific meaning assigned	May be used for any function except for buttons with the function of STOP or OFF

From IEC 73

Table 17.3 Summary of flashing and acceptance procedures for flashing lights, annunciators and digital readouts

Colour	Rapidly flashing signals (high priority)		Slowly flashing signals (lower priority)	
	Significance	On acceptance	Significance	On acceptance
Red	Urgent action required to avert danger	Audible alarm (if any) silenced. Flashing signal changes to steady signal, which persists until normal conditions return. *But* for 'Danger to personnel', audible alarm (if any) and flashing signal persist until danger is over	Not applicable	Not applicable
Yellow	Action required because of unwanted change	Audible alarm (if any) silenced. Flashing signal may be extinguished, or may continue flashing until action is taken or may change to steady signal	Lower priority unwanted change	Flashing signal changes to steady
Green	Not applicable	Not applicable	Change of state. Discrepancy from commanded state. Attention required	Flashing signal changes to steady
Blue	Not applicable	Not applicable	Change of state. Discrepancy from commanded state. Attention required	Flashing signal changes to steady
White	Non-urgent action required, e.g. change of state or discrepancy from a commanded state	Audible alarm (if any) silenced. Flashing signal may be extinguished, or may continue flashing until action is taken or may change to steady signal	Change of state. Discrepancy from commanded state. Attention required.	Flashing signal changes to steady

From BS 4099: Part 2

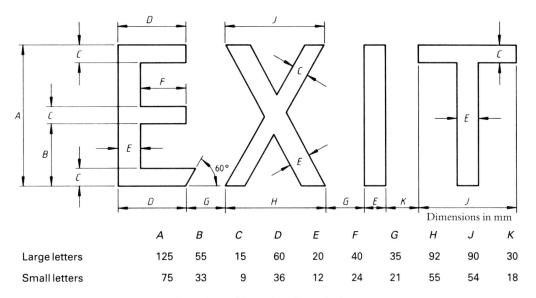

	A	B	C	D	E	F	G	H	J	K
Large letters	125	55	15	60	20	40	35	92	90	30
Small letters	75	33	9	36	12	24	21	55	54	18

Figure 17.1 Proportions and spacing of lettering for exit signs
From BS 2560

BS 4099:Part 2 recommends two standard sizes for annunciators:

	Large mm	Small mm
Minimum illuminated window area	40 × 90	20 × 33
Spacing between window centres		
—vertical	50	25
—horizontal	100	38

It further specifies that characters of the legend:
1 should have a height not less than $\frac{1}{360}$ of the maximum reading distance, i.e. $0.0028D$. (Note that this is considerably less than the character height specified in BS 3693.)

2 should have a stroke width of between $\frac{1}{6}$ and $\frac{1}{10}$ character height;
3 should have an average ratio of height to width of approximately 3:2.

Recommendations 1 and 2 also apply to digital readouts.

BS 2560 and BS 5499 deal with exit signs (internally illuminated or self-luminous respectively) for use in public auditoria. Two standard sizes are recommended with overall front panel dimensions of 412 mm × 187 mm and 267 mm × 137 mm (± 3 mm for all dimensions). Recommended proportions and spacing of lettering are shown in figure 17.1.

17.2 Digital displays

The principal varieties of digital display are:
1 electro-mechanical 'counters'—now more or less obsolete;
2 segmented numerals—usually light-emitting diodes (LEDs) or liquid crystal displays (LCDs);
3 cathode ray tube (CRT) displays as used in visual display units (VDUs);
4 large-scale dot matrix displays.

Segmented numerals

The technical advantages (and cheapness) of segmented numeral displays have resulted in their widespread use. As LCDs become available in a wider range of colours they will become yet more attractive. The seven-stroke display, commonly employed on calculators, generates a set of numerals of fair to good legibility—provided character size and spacing is generous. A fourteen-stroke display can be used to generate an alphanumeric set of fair to poor legibility.

The VDU screen

The VDU is rapidly tending to become the universal display instrument. The range of visual material which can be presented on a good quality VDU screen is, in principle at least, virtually limitless. It may include alphanumeric material; analogue material such as graphs, histograms (bar charts), pie charts, etc.; pictographic material (known in the trade as 'iconic displays'); or any combination of these. Many screens nowadays have full colour facilities. Computer display technology is progressing so rapidly that guideline recommendations can easily be out-of-date by the time they are written.

At present, two main methods are used for generating alphanumeric characters on VDU screens: the *dot matrix method* in which the characters are formed from a pattern of circular or square dots (sometimes called 'pixels') and the *grid method* which employs horizontal, vertical and oblique strokes—see figure 17.2. The former is the more common and it is probably the more legible.

At the time of writing the most detailed standard dealing with VDUs is probably DIN 66 234, extracts from which are given below. The 5×7 dot matrix specified in the standard is a minimum not an optimum. It is generally accepted that, although a 5×7 dot matrix gives a reasonably legible character set, a 7×9 or even a 9×11 matrix is preferable. Similarly, greater character spacings and character sizes than those shown in the standard are desirable. Optimum character heights are in the order of 20 minutes of arc or 4 mm at a 600 mm viewing distance.

Screens which display dark characters on a light background (positive polarity) are generally less fatiguing to read than those which have the reverse arrangement (negative polarity)—although the latter remain more common.

A further discussion of VDUs is to be found in section 10.

DIN 66 234 includes the following recommendations for the design of VDU screens.

- The character contrast (that is, the ratio of the mean luminance of a character to the mean luminance of its background) should be between 6:1 and 10:1. Contrasts below 3:1 may reduce legibility; contrasts above 15:1 may cause visual discomfort. It should be possible to adjust the contrast to suit prevailing lighting conditions.
- The font height should subtend a visual angle of at least 18 minutes (when viewed at a right angle). Since the viewing distance should not be less than 500 mm, the minimum acceptable font height is 2.6 mm.
- The width of a capital letter should be approximately 70%, but no less than 50%, of its height.

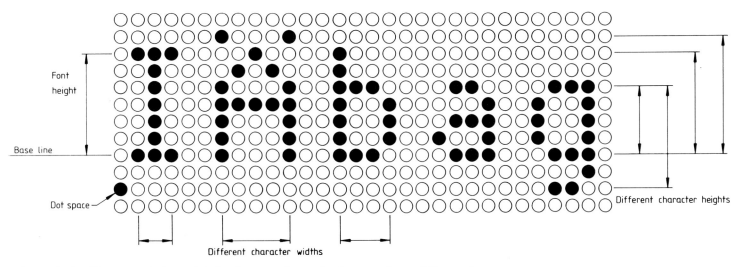

Figure 17.2a Character design with the dot-matrix method; examples and illustrations
From DIN 66 234 Part 1

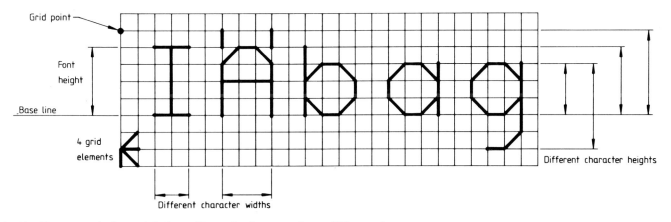

Figure 17.2b Character design with the grid method; examples and illustrations
From DIN 66 234 Part 1

- The spacing between characters should be at least one dot space or 15% of the font height or font width as the case may be. (This applies to both horizontal character spacing and vertical line spacing; in the latter case descenders must be considered.)
- Capital letters generated by the dot matrix method should be at least 7 dot spaces in height and 5 in width (except 'I').
- Capital letters generated by the grid method should be at least 5 grid points in height and 4 in width (except 'I').

17.3 Analogue displays

Despite the rapid progress of digital display technology, analogue devices remain ergonomically preferable where the operator is required to monitor or track some continuously changing variable—particularly if its value must be compared with a critical reference level.

BS 3693 is an extremely detailed set of recommendations for the design of analogue displays. It is based on sound ergonomic principles and a substantial body of empirical research which is described, for example, in Murrell (1969). Figure 17.3 explains some of the terminology which will be used in the following discussion.

In general an analogue instrument or 'dial' consists of an 'index' (which is usually a pointer) and a set of graduated marks and numbers known as a 'scale'. The standard applies both to those instruments in which an index moves in relation to a fixed scale (the more common arrangement) and to those in which the scale moves in relation to a fixed index. No recommendations are given for scales displayed on CRTs.

In most circumstances, scales with relatively few graduation marks (*open scales*) are easiest to read. Observers are capable of interpolating between graduation marks to an accuracy of $\frac{1}{5}$ of the scale division. (It has been shown that subdivision 'by eye' into more than five parts results in a substantial reduction in accuracy; but subdivision into less than five parts does not give any improvement in the number of correct readings made by an experienced observer.)

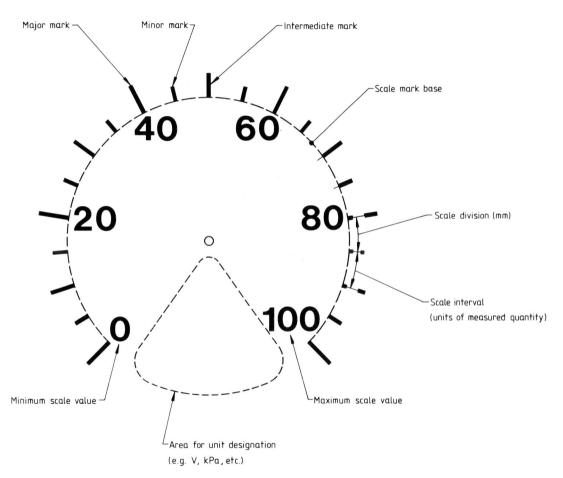

Figure 17.3 Terms for dials and scales   From BS 3693

BS 3693 defines the *interpolated resolution* of an analogue instrument as 'The smallest change in the measured or supplied quantity to which a numerical value can be assigned by interpolation, i.e. by estimating the distance between the index and the nearest scale mark'. This is expressed as a percentage of the total scale range. Interpolation to $\frac{1}{5}$ of a scale division is assumed (unless otherwise specified). The *resolution factor* (r) of an instrument is numerically equal to the interpolated resolution. Hence, if the interpolated resolution of an instrument is 0.5% of the total scale range then $r = 0.5$. In general, as speed of observation becomes more important, the required resolution factor will increase—hence, an automobile speedometer would normally have a resolution factor of about 1, whereas for laboratory test instruments a lower value may be more appropriate. The performance criterion, upon which the standard is based, is that 95% of observations, by experienced observers standing directly in front of the scale, shall be within the interpolated resolution. A minimum illuminance of 130 lx is assumed.

The proportion of observation errors, in reading an analogue instrument, depends (among many other factors) upon the angle subtended at the observer's eye by the interpolated scale division. The optimum value of this angle is considered to be 7×10^{-4} rad which is equivalent to 2.5 minutes of arc. When the angle is larger than this, the error rate increases and when the angle is less than 2.5 minutes it increases rapidly. This figure may be used to determine the overall *scale length* (L) of the instrument. (This applies equally to linear, full circle or part circle scales.)

The minimum acceptable scale length is given by the equation

$L = 0.0007 D n$

where

L is the scale length (in mm)

D is the reading distance (in mm)

and

n is the total number of interpolated divisions.

Since, by definition,

$n = 100/r$

(where r is the resolution factor)

then,

$L = 0.07 D/r$

The minimum acceptable scale length, defined by the above equations, may, with advantage, be increased by a factor of up to two. It is suggested in the standard that instruments intended for 'close reading' should be designed for a reading distance (D) of 300 mm and that for panel mounted instruments a reading distance of 1000 mm would be appropriate. Table 17.4 gives examples of scale lengths calculated from the above considerations. The relationship between reading distance and scale length is also shown in figure 17.4.

Table 17.4 Examples of scale lengths for reading at distances of 300 mm and 1000 mm

Reading distance, D	Minimum length, L, for resolution factor, r		
	$r = 0.2$	$r = 0.5$	$r = 1.0$
mm	mm	mm	mm
300	105	42	21
1000	350	140	70

From BS 3693

The required dimensions of all other scale markings may be determined from the scale length, according to the proportions given in table 17.5.

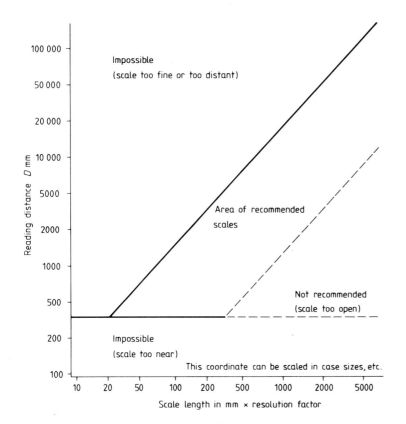

Figure 17.4 Relations between reading distance and scale length with respect to resolution factor
From BS 3693

Note. The right hand limit has been arbitrarily chosen and represents an interpolated division 10 times as large as the minimum recommended. It may be readjusted to suit manufacturing requirements.

Table 17.5 Dimensions of scaled marks expressed as a ratio to the scale length

Resolution factor		0.1 to 0.25	0.33 to 0.62	0.67 to 1.25
Minor scale mark	Thickness★	0.001	0.002 25	0.0045
	Length★	0.01	0.016	0.024
Intermediate scale mark	Thickness	As thickness of minor scale mark		
	Length	1.5 times length of minor scale mark		
Major scale mark	Thickness	As thickness of minor scale mark		
	Length	2 times length of minor scale mark		
Figure(s)	Height★	0.02	0.03	0.04

★ These dimensions should be within ± 20% of these values. The ratio of the sizes of the major and intermediate scale marks to the minor scale marks should remain as given in this table.

Note. The dimensions of scale marks are obtained by multiplying the scale length by the values shown in this table.

From BS 3693

The readability of a scale is determined, not only by the boldness of its markings, but also by the manner in which it is divided up and marked. In general, the following principles will minimize the necessity for mental calculation and hence tend to reduce operator error.

- Scale divisions should represent 1, 2 or 5 units of the measured quantity (or 10, 20, 50, etc.).
- There should never be more than four minor marks between intermediate marks; nor should there be more than four intermediate marks between major marks.
- There should not be more than four unfigured major marks between figured major marks.
- There should not be more than two unfigured marks between adjacent figured marks.

Linear scales should, wherever possible, be divided in accordance with one of the examples given in figure 17.5. Note that the interpolated resolutions given in figure 17.5 are expressed as percentages of the scale range—in some cases this implies division of the smallest scale intervals into five parts; in other cases it implies four part division.

The *pointer* which is used to indicate scale values should be designed to give maximum accuracy. Where the tip is pointed, it should overlap the scale by between one-third and two-thirds of the length of the minor scale mark. Recommended shapes for pointer tips are given in figure 17.6.

The directions in which a pointer should move, in order to indicate an increase in magnitude of the measured quantity, are shown in table 17.6. Illustrations of the types of scales are given in figure 17.7.

Other recommendations from the standard include the following:

- In general it is considered that the use of boundary lines on scales is undesirable. However, if such a line is required its edge should coincide with the base of the scale marks and its thickness should not exceed that of a minor scale mark. There should never be more than one boundary line.
- For circular and part-circular scales it is preferable that the figures should be on the outside of the scale arc so as not to be obscured by the index—but constraints of scale length and overall dial size may make this impossible.
- For straight, sector and quadrant scales, the figure should always be on the side of the scale opposite to the index. In general, figures should be on the left of vertical straight scales and above horizontal ones. (There may be exceptions—where ease of comparative reading requires scales to be mounted in opposing pairs.)
- It is recommended that for scale figures (other than the maximum scale value) the number of digits should not exceed three. This may require the use of an appropriate prefix. Hence 12 000 V could be replaced by 12 kV and 0.005 bar by 5 mbar, etc.

BS 3693 recommends that the heights of digits and unit designations should subtend an angle of at least 16 minutes of arc at the user's eye (which is equal to 0.00465 rad); the width/height ratio of the characters should be between 55 % and 80 %; the stroke width should be between 10 % and 20 % of character height; and italic forms should not be used. Examples of typical character heights are given in table 17.7.

Acceptable typefaces include Helvetica Medium, Futura Medium, Grotesque, Univers Bold, etc. Helvetica Medium has been used in figures 17.5 and 17.7. A recommended form of digits is given in BS 3693A and 3693B—see figure 17.8.

BS 3693 also includes discussion of non-linear scales, dual scales and the problems of parallax.

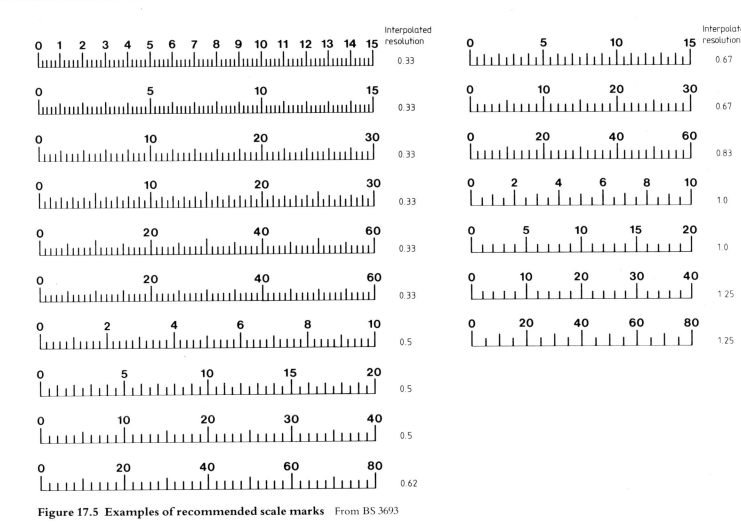

Figure 17.5 Examples of recommended scale marks   From BS 3693

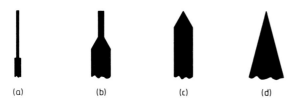

(a)   (b)   (c)   (d)

(a) is recommended for resolutions up to 0.5 and multiple scales;
(b) is recommended for resolutions from 0.5 up to, but not including, 1.0;
(c) and (d) are recommended for resolutions of 1.0 and above.

Figure 17.6 Recommended shapes of pointer tip   From BS 3693

Table 17.6 Direction of movement of the index for increasing magnitude of the measured quantity

Type of scale	Direction of movement
Circular and part circular	Clockwise
Horizontal sector (top) Horizontal sector (bottom) }	From left to right
Vertical sector (left hand)	Upwards (i.e. clockwise)
Vertical sector (right hand)	Upwards (i.e. anticlockwise)
Quadrant (upper left)	Upwards (i.e. clockwise)
Vertical, straight or edgewise	Upwards
Horizontal, straight or edgewise	From left to right

Note. Increasing magnitude includes a transition from a negative value towards zero.

From BS 3693

17.4 Layout of displays and controls

If the user of a product or a workstation is confronted with an array of displays and controls, his task will be simplified if their layout conforms to the following common-sense principles.

- The most important or frequently used displays should be in the optimal area as discussed in section 14.2.
- The most important or frequently used manual controls should be within easy reach, directly in front of the operator, between elbow and shoulder height.
- Displays and controls which have similar functions should be close together.
- Displays and controls which are operated in sequence should be close together—preferably arranged in sequence from left to right or top to bottom.
- All displays and controls should conform to motion stereotypes as discussed in section 26.1.

Additional information—Most books about ergonomics include a section on the design of visual displays. These include Murrell (1969), McCormick and Saunders (1982), Pheasant (1986, Ch 17). Discussions of visual display units include Cakir et al (1980), Ericsson (1983), HSE (1983) and Grandjean (1986).

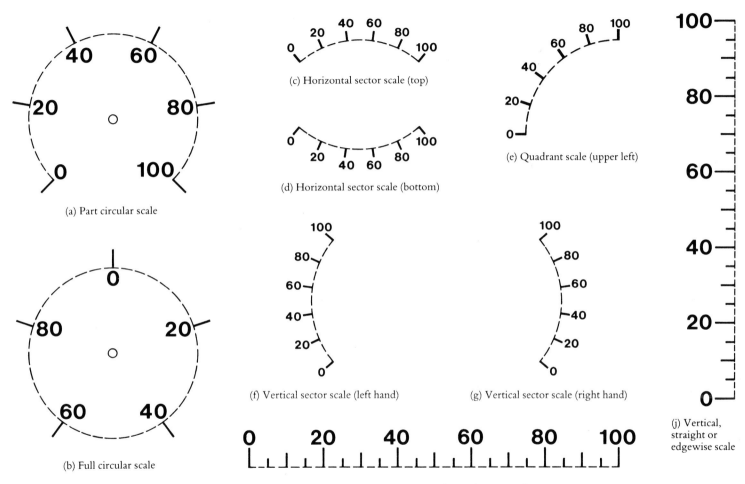

(a) Part circular scale

(b) Full circular scale

(c) Horizontal sector scale (top)

(d) Horizontal sector scale (bottom)

(e) Quadrant scale (upper left)

(f) Vertical sector scale (left hand)

(g) Vertical sector scale (right hand)

(h) Horizontal, straight or edgewise scale

(j) Vertical, straight or edgewise scale

Figure 17.7 Types of scales   From BS 3693

Table 17.7 Examples of character heights for reading at distances of 300 mm to 1000 mm

Reading distance	Character height
mm	mm
300	1.4
600	2.8
1000	4.65

From BS 3693

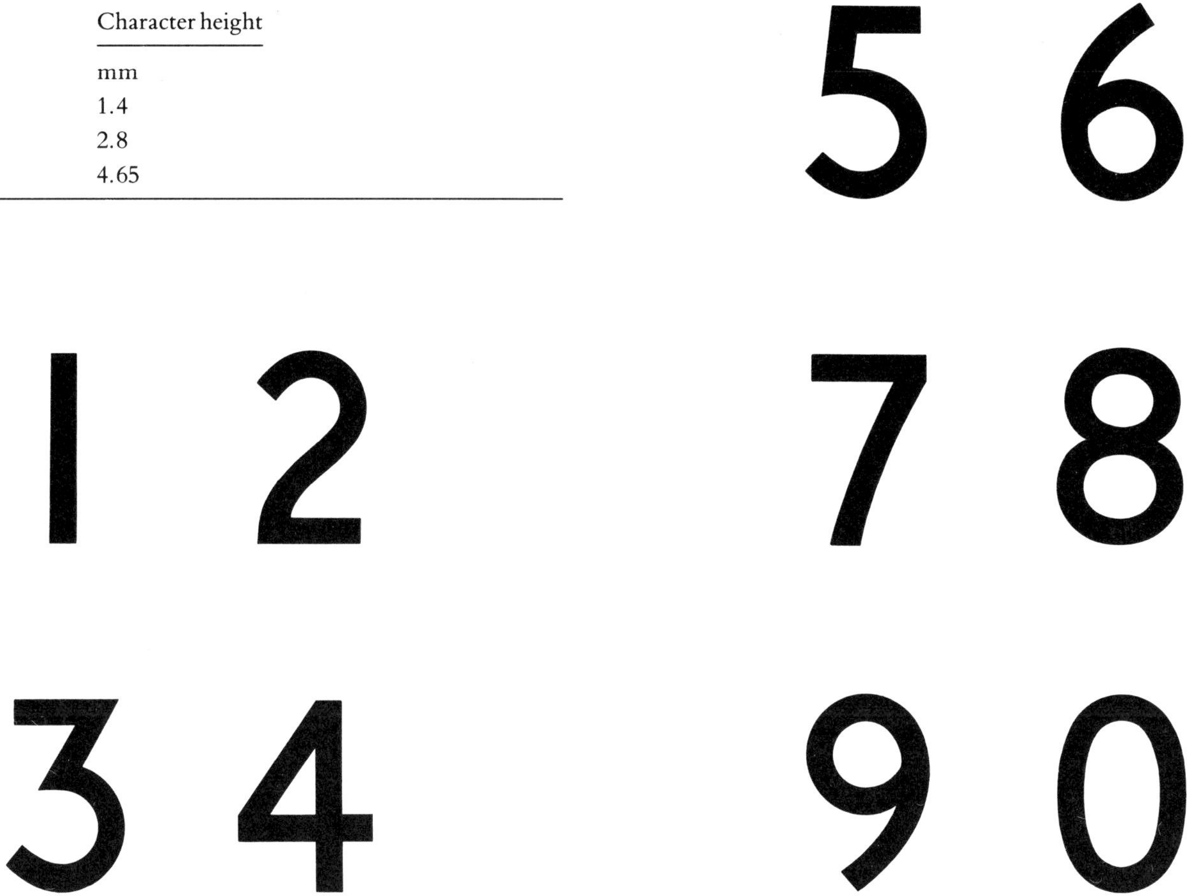

Figure 17.8 Recommended forms of digits From BS 3693A

Section 18 Prose and plain English

An earlier section (15) dealt with the *legibility* of printed text. We shall now consider some further factors which influence its *comprehensibility*—that is, the ease with which, having been *read*, it may be *understood*. We have all encountered forms which were difficult to fill in, instructions which were difficult to follow and books which 'blinded us with science' or dressed up a simple idea in needlessly complex language. How may these pitfalls be avoided? Many people, who are considered to 'write well', would admit to doing so by a process of trial and error. Indeed, to the best of my knowledge, this is the only known method. There are certain principles, however, which although they should never be treated as hard and fast rules, might reasonably be expected to shorten the trial and error process. The following comments were compiled with reference to Wright and Barnard (1975) and Hartley (1978)—but I have taken considerable liberties in modifying their recommendations to suit my own prejudices.

The clarity of a passage of text depends primarily upon the orderliness of its structure: that is, upon the logical relationship between its parts. This applies not only to the overall structure of the piece but also to the finer details of individual sentences. Within reason, the former is probably more important (particularly in scientific and technical writing). Most reasonably well-motivated readers will take the trouble to puzzle out the occasional clumsy sentence or unfamiliar word; but they will be much less tolerant of writing which is muddled on a larger scale. When ideas follow one another without their connections being made explicit, the typical reader just gives up. The writer who cannot be bothered to construct a logical framework for his ideas, can scarcely expect his readers to construct one for themselves.

Any text which is more than a few sentences in length, requires to be broken down into sections, sub-sections, paragraphs, etc. Sometimes (but certainly not always) it is helpful to number these. As far as possible, the divisions of the passage should accurately reflect the divisions of its argument. If this has been achieved then the divisions should be reinforced by the appropriate use of space and by setting headings and sub-headings in type of varied size and boldness. (Scientific text books are sometimes laid out very badly in this respect.) Hartley (1978) recommends that the commencement of a paragraph should be indentified by a line spacing, rather than an indention and that multiples of a line space should be used for larger subdivisions.

The reader's attention may be drawn to critical features of the text in a number of ways. Passages may be indented, set in larger type, or placed in a box. All these methods are similarly effective. The use of marginal comments may be valuable (in my opinion) but they are somewhat archaic. Marks such as '•' or '□' are becoming increasingly common.

Vocabulary is a slightly vexed question. We are often advised to 'stick to plain English' or to 'avoid jargon'. If all else is equal, this is obviously good sense—especially when writing for the general public. But one man's jargon is another person's technical terminology and the specialized vocabularies of trades and professions sometimes evolve for perfectly good reasons—not just the desire to confuse and mystify outsiders. Deciding where to draw the line is a matter of fine judgement and the commonest word is only best where it may be used just as precisely as any of its rarer rivals. The worst problems arise where the technical meaning of a particular word differs from its everyday meaning. The simplest solution is to define words that are likely to cause confusion.

The following commonly quoted principles are said to distinguish easy sentences from difficult ones. In general, it is true that:

— short sentences (with few clauses) are easier to understand than long ones;
— the active form of a statement is easier to understand than the passive;
— positive statements (particularly instructions) are easier to understand than negatives.

All of these 'rules' have exceptions. The real difficulty with long sentences is not only due to the number of words, or even the number of clauses. As a sentence increases in length its structural integrity tends to be lost. This occurs particularly when a verb is widely separated from its subject or object. But quite complex structures can sometimes be the most efficient. Subordinate clauses may eliminate repetition or the potentially ambiguous use of personal pronouns and may help to alleviate the staccato quality that deliberately simplified writing tends to acquire. Passives are entirely appropriate where it is necessary or desirable to avoid mentioning the agent of a verb—hence, we might say 'this chair was designed for comfort'. In formal scientific writing the desire for anonymity has become a stylistic fetish. Negative statements also have a perfectly valid role—there is no obvious alternative to a prohibition like 'please do not walk on the grass'.

On the whole I do not find rules or guidelines for writing to be particularly helpful. In attempting to characterize good prose we tend to use terms like 'structure' or 'rhythm'. These qualities are difficult to define but relatively easy to recognize. The art of writing is very much concerned with learning to recognize them and hence to bring the trial and error process to a satisfactory conclusion. The best way of ensuring that a passage is intelligible is to try it out on a representative sample of readers.

Additional information—There are many books which offer guidance on writing good English. *Fowler's Modern English Usage* (Fowler 1983) is a classic which no writer should be without. *The Oxford Guide to English Usage* and *The Oxford Dictionary for Writers and Editors* are also extremely helpful. These three books are generally considered to define 'good practice' at the present time. See also Wright and Barnard (1975), Hartley (1978) and PD6501: The preparation of British Standards for building and civil engineering: Part 2 Guide to presentation.

Part Four
Products and spaces

Section 19 Modular coordination

The topic of *modular coordination* falls outside the subject area of ergonomics as most people would define it. However, since the concept has been extensively applied to the standardization of many of the products with which the ergonomist is legitimately concerned, it is necessary to discuss it briefly here.

The principles of modular coordination are applicable not only to the structural elements of buildings, but also to the spaces which these structures define and to the furniture and other products which are placed within these spaces. (It is the spaces and products which concern the ergonomist.)

Relevant British Standards and related publications include: BS 6100, PD 6446, DD 22.

BS 6750, which deals with modular coordination in building, is a combination of, and is technically equivalent to ISO 1006, ISO 1040, ISO 2848, ISO 6511, ISO 6512, ISO 6513 and ISO 6514. Other related standards and documents include ISO 1791, ISO 2776 and ISO 2777.

The system defined in these standards is based on the *international basic module* of 100 mm which is denoted by the symbol M. Standard multiples of M are known as *multimodules* and standard subdivisions are known as *submodules*.

The multimodules for the coordinating dimensions of buildings are 3M, 6M, 12M, 15M, 30M and 60M. These define a series of preferred sizes, shown in table 19.1 which is to be found in both BS 6750 and ISO 6513.

BS 6750 includes specifications for modular sizes for various horizontal and vertical coordinating dimensions of spaces. These are mainly multiples of 3M or 1M and it is stated that the former is generally preferable.

Submodular increments may be used when there is a need for an increment smaller than the basic module. The first preference is M/2 = 50 mm. The second preference is M/4 = 25 mm.

Hence we may summarize the system by saying that, in choosing the dimensions of spaces or components, preference should be given to a multiple of the largest member of the following series which is compatible with functional and practical requirements:

60M, 30M, 15M, 12M, 6M, 3M, M, M/2, M/4

Comment—The goals of modular coordination are compatible with those of ergonomics to the extent that they promote the orderly and systematic arrangements of objects and spaces in buildings. They are incompatible if the dimensions of these objects and spaces are chosen with reference to an arbitrary system of 'preferences' without due consideration for the human user.

In reality the conflict is likely to be minimal—since there are relatively few situations in which it is necessary, for ergonomic reasons, to specify a dimension to an accuracy of more than 25 mm or 50 mm. In general, it is acceptable to round clearances *up* to the nearest 'preferred' value and to round reaches *down*.

Table 19.1 Series of preferred multimodular sizes for horizontal dimensions

Multimodules					
3M	6M	12M	15M	30M	60M
3M					
6M	6M				
9M					
12M	12M	12M			
15M			15M		
18M	18M				
21M					
24M	24M	24M			
27M					
30M	30M		30M	30M	
33M					
36M	36M	36M			
39M					
42M	42M				
45M			45M		
48M	48M	48M			
	54M				
	60M	60M	60M	60M	60M
	66M				
	72M	72M			
			75M		
	78M				
	84M	84M			
	90M		90M	90M	
	96M	96M			
			105M		
		108M			
		120M	120M	120M	120M
		etc.	etc.	etc.	etc.

From ISO 6513

Section 20 Circulation and access in buildings

20.1 General

Space requirements for general purposes, such as hallways, corridors, lobbies and other circulation areas in buildings, are summarized in table 20.1. They are based principally on Tutt and Adler (1979) and Noble (1982). Unless otherwise specified, dimensions should allow restricted access for a 95th %le adult man. Restricted figures might be expected to cause a degree of inconvenience (Noble 1982). Note that certain figures given in ISO 3055 are equal to these 'restricted' values.

Corridors, etc. should generally allow two people walking one way to pass a third person walking the other way without crowding or jostling—a clearance of 2100 mm is required for this purpose.

20.2 Walking

The data given in table 20.2 are calculated (for an average adult of 1675mm stature) from the equation:

$$\frac{\text{length of pace/stature}}{\text{step frequency (per min)}} = 0.004$$

which is quoted by Inman et al (1981)

Men and women will characteristically use slightly different combinations of pace length and step frequency to achieve the same walking speed. The extreme categories (very slow and very fast) will rarely be encountered in practice. A 'comfortable' walking speed, which minimizes energy expenditure, is probably a little less than the average value in the table.

Table 20.1 Space requirements in corridors, hallways and other circulation areas Dimensions in mm

Widths of access

One person walking normally	650 (600 restricted)[1]
Two people passing or walking side by side	1350 (1200 restricted)[1]
Two people passing crabwise	900 (850 restricted)[1]
One person walking, another flattened against wall	1000 (900 restricted)[1]
One person carrying a suitcase	800
One person carrying a tea-tray	900
One person carrying two suitcases	1000
One person with a raised umbrella	1150
Two people with raised umbrellas	2350
One person with crutches	840
One person with walking frame	1000
Wheelchair user — minimum	750[2]
— reasonable	800[1,2]
— preferred	900

Passage between obstacles	**Normal**	**Crabwise**
Both obstacles greater than 1000 mm in height	650	400
One obstacle greater than 1000 mm in height; the other less	600	400
Both obstacles less than 1000 mm in height	550	350

Standing in line	450 per person

Floorspace allowances for standing/walking	**m²/person**
General design purposes	0.8
Relatively free circulation	1.2
Standing in a crowd (moderate density)	0.5 to 0.65
Shuffling forward	0.3 to 0.4
Standing under very crowded conditions (acceptable for short periods only)	0.2 to 0.3

Data compiled from various sources including Tutt and Adler (1979), Noble (1982), Pheasant (1986).
Notes 1. See also ISO 3055
      2. See also BS 5619 and BS 5810

Table 20.2 Walking: tempo, pace and speed for a typical adult

	Tempo	Length of pace	Speed	
	Steps/min	mm	m/s	miles/h
Very slow	60	400	0.4	0.9
Slow	80	540	0.72	1.6
Average	110	740	1.36	3.0
Fast	130	870	1.89	4.2
Very fast	150	870	2.18	4.9

Note. 1 mile/h = 0.447 m/s

20.3 Stairs

Changes of level in buildings may be achieved using ramps, stairs or ladders according to the pitch (angle of ascent from the horizontal). In general a ramp will be used for pitches less than 15°; stairs for pitches of 15° to 55°; and ladders for pitches greater than 55°. In terms of physiological efficiency the optimum pitch for a staircase is about 30°. Circumstances will commonly demand a steeper ascent.

BS 5395 deals with the design of stairs, ladders and walkways (Part 1 for straight stairs and Part 2 spiral or helical stairs). Terminology used is shown in figure 20.1.

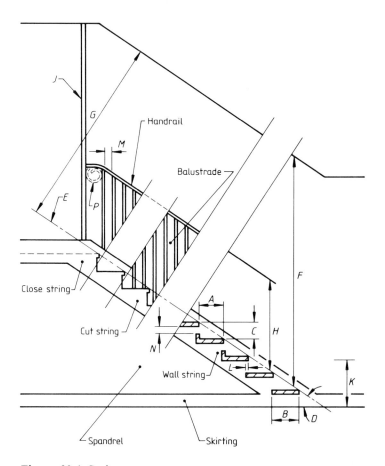

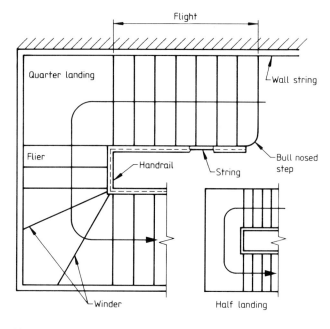

Key

A	going	**J**	storey post
B	tread depth	**K**	handrail required where stair
C	rise		rises more than 600 mm
D	pitch	**L**	overlap
E	pitch line	**M**	gaps in balustrades
F	headroom	**N**	openings between adjacent
G	clearance		treads
H	balustrade height	**P**	scroll or returned end

Figure 20.1 Stair terms
From BS 5395: Part 1

Tread, rise and pitch

The depth of tread should be adequate to support the foot and allow at least part of the heel to rest firmly on each step (without placing the foot at an angle). The horizontal distance between the edge (or *nosing*) of one step and the next is called the *going*. In general, the going should be between 250 mm and 300 mm.

Steps with an excessively shallow rise (less than 70 mm) increase the risk of tripping. A rise of more than about 230 mm is too great to negotiate in comfort.

In order to give a comfortable length of pace, it is assumed that:

twice riser + going = 550 mm to 700 mm
(optimum value approximately 600 mm)

Within reasonable limits, the flatter the pitch the safer the stairs. Therefore stairs used in public places or by the elderly or infirm should have a shallower pitch than those used in private dwellings or by the able bodied. (Recommendations for disabled users are given in table 21.1.)

Recommendations for combinations of the above variables are given in figure 20.2 and in table 20.3.

In general, there should not be fewer than three or more than 16 risers in any one flight. (Between the external door of a building and the ground, and at the foot of a stair serving a single dwelling, one or two risers are permitted.) In public places there should not be more than two flights without a change in direction (or one flight if it has more than 12 steps).

The going and riser should be equal for each step in a flight. Winders should be avoided wherever possible and should not be used in public places.

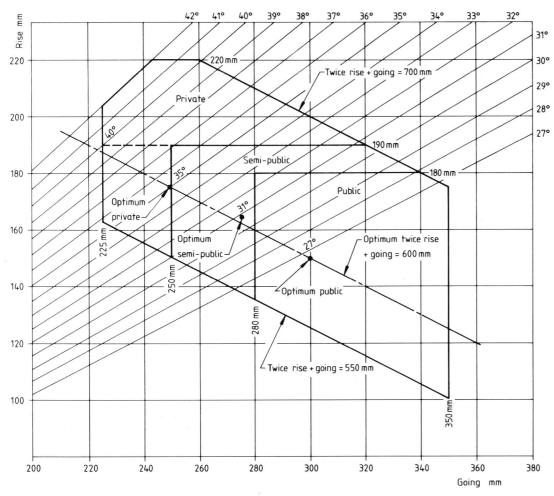

Notes.
1. Within the outlines shown any combination of rise and going falls within the limiting dimensions.

2. The public outline includes semi-public and private.

3. The semi-public outline includes private

4. Preferred combinations of rise and going are those which lie nearest the 2 r + g = 600 mm line.

5. The three optima indicated are those based on goings of 250 mm, 275 mm and 300 mm.

Figure 20.2 Relationship between rise/going/pitch limitations
From BS 5395: Part 1

Table 20.3 Dimensions for stairs   Dimensions in mm

Stair	Rise			Going			Sum twice rise + going			Pitch		Clear width (see note 2)	
	Min.	Optimum	Max.	Min.	Optimum	Max.	Min.	Optimum	Max.	Optimum	Max.	Min.	Reduced minimum where stair has limited use
Private stair★	100	175	190 desirable 220 absolute maximum	225	250	350	550	600	700	35°	40° desirable 42° absolute maximum	800	600
Semi-public stair†	100	165	190	250	275	350	550	600	700	31°	38°	1000	800
Public stair‡	100	150	180	280	300	350	550	600	700	27°	33°	1000 (hospitals 1200)	See note 4

★ Stair used by a limited number of people who are generally very familiar with the stair, e.g., the internal stair in a dwelling.

† Stair used by larger numbers of people, some of whom may be unfamiliar with the stair, e.g., in factories, offices, shops, common stair serving more than one dwelling.

‡ Stair used by large numbers of people at one time, e.g., in places of public assembly. Stair used by people with ambulatory difficulties, e.g., in hospitals, children's homes.

Notes.

1. Special circumstances may demand easier limiting dimensions than some of those given in the table.

2. The dimensions in these columns relate to clear width, i.e. clear of handrails and other obstructions. Requirements for means of escape in case of fire may require a greater minimum than indicated, and where means of escape is a factor the relevant mandatory regulations should be consulted.

3. The limiting dimensions in each column apply to the stair as a whole so that the most onerous requirement should be complied with in each case. Thus, for example, in the private stair the minimum going cannot be used with the maximum rise in view of the pitch limitation. The relationship between the rise/going/pitch limitations is illustrated in figure 20.2.

4. A reduced minimum clear width is not appropriate to this type of stair in view of its stated use.

Recommendations for *headroom and clearance* are shown in figure 20.3.

For short flights of three or four steps the clearance should be increased to 1800 mm (since boisterous young people are prone to take these at a running jump).

Guarding of stairs and landings

According to BS 5395, balustrades (or other similar barriers to falling) should extend a vertical distance of at least 840 mm above the pitch line for stairs within a single dwelling and at least 900 mm elsewhere. For the edges of landings a barrier of at least 900 mm is required in a single dwelling and 1100 mm elsewhere.

Comment—Barriers of 840 mm and 900 mm are somewhat risky and 1100 mm would probably be better.

In buildings frequented by small children, gaps in balustrades, etc., should not be large enough to permit the passage of a sphere of 100 mm diameter, and should not provide toe-holds for climbing.

Handrail

The handrail should be fixed at a vertical height of between 840 mm and 1000 mm above the pitch line. If the stair is more than 1000 mm in width, there should be a handrail on each side. The handrail which provides the most comfortable grip is circular in cross-section with a diameter of 45 mm to 50 mm.

Surface finish

In general, the coefficient of friction (μ) between shoes and floor, should be at least 0.4. For the nosings of stairs in public buildings a coefficient of friction of 0.75 is desirable (and 0.6 is the minimum acceptable).

Table 20.4 shows the frictional characteristics of some common floor finishes.

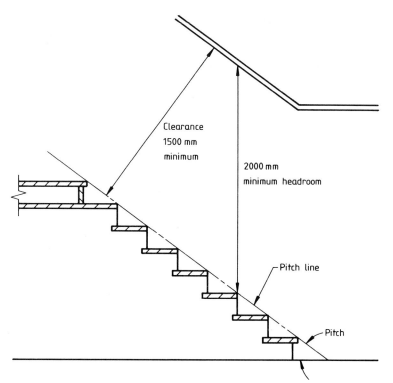

Figure 20.3 Headroom on stairs From BS 5395: Part 1

Table 20.4 Slip resistance of floor and tread finishes

Material	Slip resistance★		Remarks
	Dry and unpolished	Wet	
Clay tiles (carborundum finish)	very good	very good	May be suitable for external stairs
Carpet	very good	good	
Clay tiles (textured)	very good	good	May be suitable for external stairs
Cork tiles	very good	good	
PVC with non-slip granules	very good	good	
PVC	very good	poor to fair	Slip resistance when wet may be improved if PVC is textured. Edges of sheet liable to cause tripping if not fixed firmly to base
Rubber (sheets or tiles)	very good	very poor	Not suitable near entrance doors
Mastic asphalt	good	good	
Vinyl asbestos tiles	good	fair	
Linoleum	good	poor to fair	Edges of sheets may cause tripping if not securely fixed to base
Concrete	good	poor to fair	If a textured finish or a non-slip aggregate is used, slip resistance value when wet may be increased to good
Granolithic	good	poor to fair	Slip resistance when wet may be improved to good by incorporating carborundum finish
Cast iron	good	poor to fair	Slip resistance may be acceptable when wet if open treads used
Clay tiles	good	poor to fair	Slip resistance when wet and polished very poor
Terrazzo	good	poor to fair	Non-slip nosing necessary on stairs. Slip resistance when polished or if polish is transferred by shoes from adjacent surfaces very poor

μ = coefficient of friction
★'Very good' means surface suitable for areas where special care is required, approximates to $\mu > 0.75$
  'Good' means surface satisfactory for normal use, approximates to μ 0.4 to < 0.75
  'Poor to fair' means surface below acceptable safety limits, approximates to μ 0.2 to < 0.4
  'Very poor' means surface unsafe, approximates to $\mu < 0.2$
From BS 5395: part 1

20.4 Escalators and passenger conveyors

BS 5656 (which is also EN 115) deals with the safety of escalators (i.e. moving staircases) and passenger conveyors (i.e. moving walkways, usually in the form of pallets or a belt). Its extremely detailed specifications include the following:

- Specifications concerning the angle of inclination (measured from the horizontal) and the approach to landings are summarized in table 20.5.

- Unrestricted areas for the accommodation of passengers shall be provided at landings. These shall be at least 2.5 m in depth (measured from the end of the balustrade) and equal in width to the distance between handrail centrelines; or at least 2.0 m in depth and equal in width to double the distance between handrail centrelines. Clear height shall not be less than 2.3 m.

- Lighting on escalators and conveyors shall give an illumination at the landing of not less than 50 lx indoors or 15 lx outdoors, measured at floor level.

- The riser shall not exceed 240 mm. If the escalator is to be used as an emergency exit, when out of service, the riser shall not exceed 210 mm. The tread depth shall not be less than 380 mm.

- The nominal width of the step shall not be less than 580 mm and shall not exceed 1100 mm. (Greater widths are permitted for conveyors with an inclination of 6° or less.)

- The following notices for the user shall be fixed in the vicinity of the entrance to the escalator or conveyor:
  (a) 'Small children must be held firmly';
  (b) 'Dogs must be carried';
  (c) 'Stand facing the direction of travel; keep feet away from sides';
  (d) 'Hold the handrail'.

Wherever possible these should be presented in the form of pictographs.

- The standard includes a large number of other technical and dimensional details.

Table 20.5 Specifications for escalators and passenger conveyors

Type	Angle of inclination (max; degrees)	Distance $D^{(1)}$ (min; metres)	Radius $R^{(2)}$ (min; metres)
Escalator			
Overall rise ≤ 6 m and rated speed ≤ 0.5 m/s	35	0.8	$1.0^{(3)}$
Overall rise > 6 m or rated speed > 0.5 m/s	30	1.2	$1.5^{(3)}$
Public service escalators rated speed > 0.65 m/s	35	$1.6^{(4)}$	2.6 upper end$^{(4)}$ 2.0 lower end$^{(4)}$
Passenger conveyor	12	$0.6^{(5)}$	$0.4^{(5)}$

Notes.
1. D is the minimum distance for which the supporting surface is moving horizontally at landings
2. R is the minimum radius of curvature of the transition between incline and horizontal at landings
3. Rise not relevant in determining this minimum
4. These are described as 'permitted' increases
5. Applies to conveyors with incline of more than 6°
   Radius requirement only applies to belt conveyors

From BS 5656

20.5 Lifts

BS 5655 deals with lifts and service lifts. Part 5 includes specifications for the dimensions of the following types of electric lift installation.

(a) *light passenger* (as in hotels, small offices, etc. and residential buildings);

(b) *residential* (for passengers in residential buildings only);

(c) *general purpose passenger* (for banks, office buildings, hotels, etc.);

(d) *intensive passenger traffic* (as for (c) where the travel is normally greater than 30 m);

(e) *bed/passenger* (for hospitals, nursing homes, residential houses and similar institutions);

(f) *general purpose goods* (for goods and passengers in factories, industrial plants, warehouses, etc.);

(g) *heavy duty goods* (as for (f)).

Types a, c, and d have two-panel, centre-opening, sliding doors; type b has single-panel, side-opening, sliding doors; type e has two-panel, side-opening, sliding doors; type f has collapsible, sliding, shutter doors on landing and car; type g has vertical, bi-parting, landing doors and vertical, sliding-panel, car doors. All

Table 20.6 Dimensions of lifts

Rated load (kg)	Number of passengers	Internal dimensions of car (mm)			Clear entrance (mm)		Type of installation (see text)						
		Width	Depth	Height	Width	Height	a	b	c	d	e	f	g
400	5	1100	950	2200	800	2000	●						
500	6	1100	1200	2000	1100	2000						●	
630	8	1100	1400	2200	800	2000	●	●	●				
800	10	1350	1400	2200	800	2000	●		●				
1000	13	1100	2100	2200	800	2000	●	●					
1000	13	1600	1400	2300	1100	2100			●	●			
1000	13	1400	1800	2000	1400	2000						●	
1250	16	1950	1400	2300	1100	2100			●	●			
1500	20	1700	2000	2300	1700	2300						●	●
1600	21	1950	1750	2300	1100	2100			●	●			
1600	21	1400	2400	2300	1300	2100					●		
2000	26	1500	2700	2300	1300	2100					●		
2000	26	1700	2500	2300	1700	2300						●	●
2000	26	2000	2100	2300	2000	2300						●	●

Note. The standard also specifies larger lifts in type categories e, f, and g.

From BS 5655: Part 5

doors are power operated except type f.

Selected dimensions for these types are given in table 20.6. The standard also includes well dimensions, machine-room dimensions, rated speeds, etc. The criterion relating rated load to number of passengers is defined in Part 1 of the standard. To prevent overloading by passengers the relationship between the rated load and maximum available area is given in table 20.7. The maximum number of passengers is calculated by using the formula rated load/75 and the result rounded down to the nearest whole number, or table 20.8, whichever gives the smaller value.

With the exception of the 400 kg light passenger lift, all are considered to accommodate wheelchair users.

Comment—It is worth noting that approximately 50% of adult men and 12% of adult women are heavier than 75 kg.

Table 20.7 Relationship between rated load and maximum available car area

Rated load (kg)	Maximum available car area (m^2)	Rated load (kg)	Maximum available car area (m^2)
100[1]	0.37	900	2.20
180[2]	0.58	975	2.35
225	0.70	1000	2.40
300	0.90	1050	2.50
375	1.10	1125	2.65
400	1.17	1200	2.80
450	1.30	1250	2.90
525	1.45	1275	2.95
600	1.60	1350	3.10
630	1.66	1425	3.25
675	1.75	1500	3.40
750	1.90	1600	3.56
800	2.00	2000	4.20
825	2.05	2500[3]	5.00

Notes.
1. Minimum for 1 person lift
2. Minimum for 2 person lift
3. Beyond 2500 kg add 0.16 m^2 for each extra 100 kg.

Table 20.8 Relationship between number of passengers and available car area

Number of passengers	Minimum available car area (m^2)	Number of passengers	Minimum available car area (m^2)
1	0.28	11	1.87
2	0.49	12	2.01
3	0.60	13	2.15
4	0.79	14	2.29
5	0.98	15	2.43
6	1.17	16	2.57
7	1.31	17	2.71
8	1.45	18	2.85
9	1.59	19	2.99
10	1.73	20	3.13

Beyond 20 passengers add 0.115 m^2 for each extra passenger.

From BS 5655: Part 1

From BS 5655: Part 1

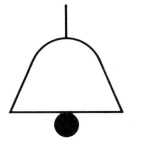

a) Alarm symbol

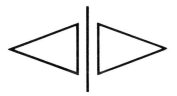

b) Door open symbol

c) Telephone or intercom symbol

d) Up direction symbol

e) Down direction symbol

Part 7 of BS 5655 deals with manual controls, indicators and other fittings. It includes the following specifications:

● The highest control device should be no more than 1800 mm above floor level.

● For independent use by people in wheelchairs, controls should be between 900 mm and 1200 mm above floor level. Such devices in the car, including the alarm button, shall be placed on a side wall at least 400 mm distant from the front and back walls. If the doors are side-opening they should be placed on the wall towards which the doors close.

● Handrails should be approximately 900 mm from the floor and have at least 20 mm clearance from the wall.

● The standard also includes lists of required controls, together with specifications for their colours and legends. Examples of symbols suitable for labelling purposes are given in figure 20.4.

Figure 20.4 Examples of symbols for use on control devices and indicators in lifts
From BS 5655: Part 7

Section 21 Requirements of disabled users of buildings

21.1 Standard recommendations

BS 5619 and BS 5810 are concerned with the special requirements of disabled people, who are defined for the purposes of the latter standard as 'people with a physical, hearing or sight impairment which affects their mobility or their use of buildings'. In many respects the term 'disabled' is invidious; unfortunately the English language lacks a better alternative. In general, it is necessary to consider the requirements both of wheelchair users and of disabled people who are able to walk (albeit with difficulty and perhaps only with the aid of crutches, frames or other supporting devices). In many cases it will be necessary to balance the requirements of a small minority of users with disabilities against those of the able-bodied majority.

BS 5619 is specifically concerned with housing, BS 5810 with access to public buildings. Recommendations overlap, both with each other and with the standards cited in section 20. Some extracts concerned principally with clearance and circulation, are given in table 21.1.

Figure 21.5 taken from BS 5810 shows the design of a lavatory which will be accessible to wheelchair users (who may be attended by helpers). (The overall dimensions are the minimum considered suitable for such purposes.)

Figure 21.6 shows a lavatory suitable for ambulant disabled people. BS 5619 also makes recommendations concerning bathrooms, bedrooms and kitchens.

Switches, telephones and other hand operated controls should not be located more than 1400 mm above floor level (BS 5810). Light switches should be aligned with door handles (1040 mm above

floor). Electrical socket outlets should not be less than 300 mm above floor level (BS 5619).

The standard symbol used to indicate a facility (such as an access route, lavatory or parking place) which is suitable for disabled people, is shown in figure 21.7.

21.2 General comments and recommendations

Standard side-hung doors (as described in BS 4787) give a clear opening width which is approximately 125 mm less than the specified size of the doorset (provided of course that obstructions do not prevent them from opening through the full 90°). Hence, a 1000 mm door will be suitable for wheelchair users in virtually all circumstances; a 900 mm door will be satisfactory in most cases and an 800 mm door will just allow a wheelchair to pass with minimal leeway (although it will conform neither to BS 5619 nor to BS 5810). The 900 mm door leaves just 300 mm side clearance (as shown in figure 21.4) in a 1200 mm passageway.

Given unobstructed access (generally to the side rather than straight ahead) an object placed between 500 mm and 1400 mm above the floor will be within tolerably convenient reach for around 95 % of those wheelchair users who do not have any additional disability which affects the mobility of the upper limbs. The preferred range of heights for controls, etc. is from around 750 mm to 1250 mm and the optimal height is around 1000 mm.

The turning circle of a wheelchair is between 1500 mm and 1700 mm in diameter.

Additional information — Pheasant (1986, Ch 10) is a general discussion of the problems of designing for people with disabilities. It includes a table of anthropometric estimates for wheelchair users. Goldsmith (1976) is generally considered definitive.

Table 21.1 Provisions for disabled users of buildings

	Public buildings (BS 5810)	Housing (BS 5619)
Approach	At least one entrance level or ramped	Preferably level; failing that, ramped
Dropped kerbs	Minimum width 1400 mm Maximum gradient 1:10	
Ramps		
Mimimum width	1200 mm	1000 mm
Maximum gradient	1:12 ($\approx 5°$)	1:12 ($\approx 5°$)
For gradients between 1:12 and 1:20	Level platform required at the head of the ramp at least 1200 mm × 1200 mm	Level platform required at the head of the ramp at least 1000 width x 1200 mm long
For gradients between 1:15 and 1:12	Handrail required	Unbroken length should not be greater than 10 m
Steps (additional to ramped approach)	Goings not less than 280 mm Risers not more than 150 mm (both should be uniform) Vertical rise not more than 1200 mm Handrail as shown in figure 21.1	
Entrance doors	Minimum clear opening of 800 mm (revolving doors not suitable) Minimum dimensions of entrance lobbies as shown in figure 21.2	Minimum clear opening 750 mm Raised thresholds not more than 25 mm Hung to facilitate wheelchair use (see figure 21.3)
Internal doors	Minimum clear opening width 750 mm Clear space at side of 300 mm (see figure 21.3) Minimum dimensions of lobbies as in figure 21.4 for single doors or figure 21.2 for double doors Door handle approximately 1040 mm above floor. Lever handles preferred	Mimimum clear opening width 770 mm Hung to facilitate wheelchairs (see figure 21.3) Door handle as for public buildings
Internal staircases	Goings not less than 250 mm Risers not higher than 170 mm Vertical rise of a flight not more than 1800 mm Handrails as in figure 21.1	Handrails as in figure 21.1
Lifts		
Internal size of car	1400 mm depth × 1100 mm width	
Doors	Clear opening width 800 mm	
Clear space in front of doors	1500 mm × 1500 mm	
Controls	Not higher than 1400 mm above floor; touch controls preferred; identifiable by blind people (e.g. embossed digits)	
Passageways	Minimum width 1200 mm	Minimum unobstructed width of 900 mm (wider preferred where practicable). Attention should be given to placing of radiators, etc.

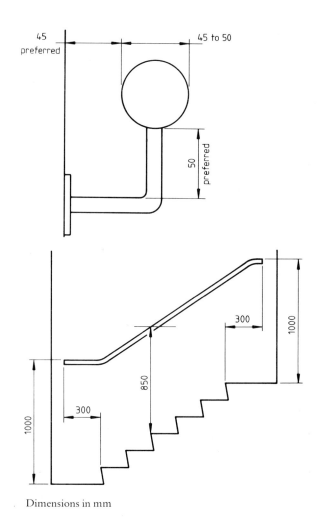

Dimensions in mm

Figure 21.1 Stair handrails and balustrades
From BS 5619

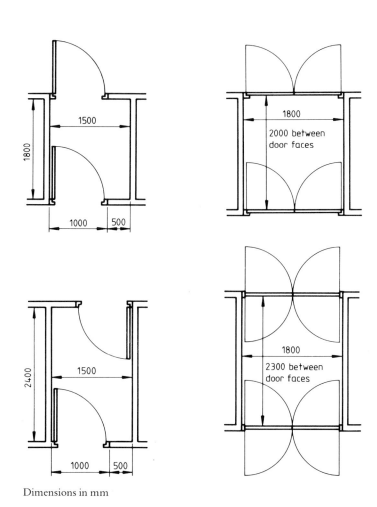

Dimensions in mm

Figure 21.2 Entrance lobbies
From BS 5810

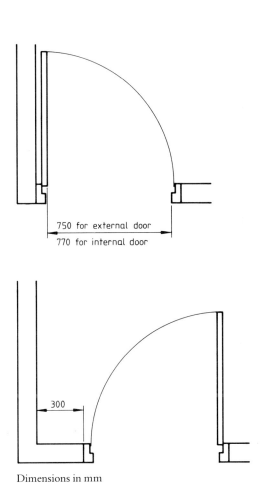

Dimensions in mm

Figure 21.3 Door openings
From BS 5619

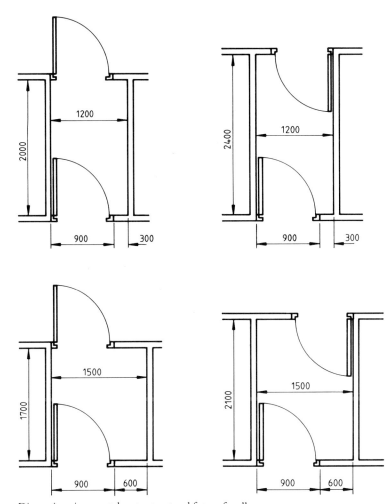

Dimensions in mm, taken to structural faces of walls

Figure 21.4 Lobbies
From BS 5810

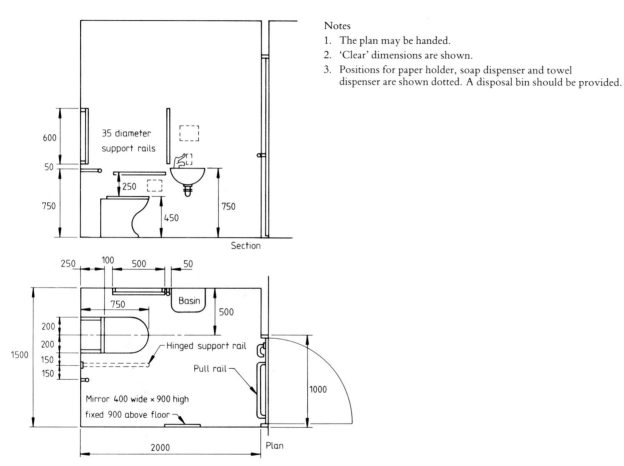

Notes
1. The plan may be handed.
2. 'Clear' dimensions are shown.
3. Positions for paper holder, soap dispenser and towel dispenser are shown dotted. A disposal bin should be provided.

Dimensions in mm

Figure 21.5 WC compartment for wheelchair users
From BS 5810

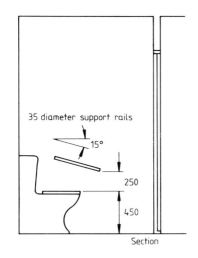

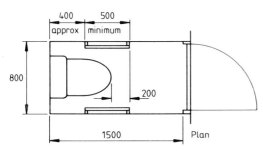

Dimensions in mm
Note. 'Clear' dimensions are shown

Figure 21.6 WC compartment for ambulant disabled
From BS 5810

Figure 21.7 Symbol for signplates indicating facilities for disabled
From BS 5810

Section 22 Tables and chairs

22.1 General principles of seat design

The basic size and shape of any seat should be determined largely by anthropometric considerations. These are discussed for seats in general in PP 7310 and Pheasant (1986) and for office furniture in BS 3044. A brief summary follows (see also section 6.1).

- *Seat height* should not be greater than the popliteal height of a small user (e.g. 5th %le).

- *Seat depth* (i.e. from the front edge to the backrest) should not be greater than the buttock-popliteal length of a small user (e.g. 5th %le).

- *Seat breadth between arm rests* should give clearance for a large user (95th %le hip breadth or elbow-elbow breadth plus leeway).

- *Without arm rests* seat breadth may be a little less than hip breadth.

- *The backrest* should be designed to support the weight of the user's trunk. This means that, in *almost all* cases, it should extend upwards, at least into the shoulder region of the user. A pad in the user's lumbar region (approximately 230 mm above the seat surface) is commonly advantageous but this should not be too pronounced.

- *The backrest angle* should be determined by the purpose of the seat. An angle of 100° to 110° from the horizontal will generally be suitable for working chairs and 110° to 120° for rest chairs. The *seat surface* should be horizontal in a working chair or tilted backwards (by an angle of 5° to 10°) in a rest chair.

Recommendations concerning writing desks and chairs are summarized in figure 22.1. (Although BS 5873, from which this figure is quoted, is concerned with school furniture, these recommendations are equally relevant in other contexts.) Not all ergonomists would agree with recommendation E; many would consider that the desk top should be above elbow level (in adults by around 50 mm).

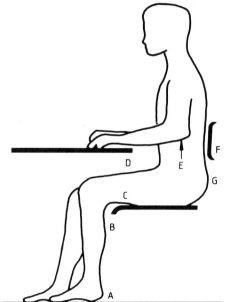

A   Shod feet flat on floor.
B   Clearance between back of legs and front edge of seat.
C   No pressure at front of seat between seating surface and thighs.
D   Clearance between thigh and underside of table for freedom of movement.
E   Elbows approximately level with table top when upper arm vertical.
F   Firm support for back in lumbar region and below shoulder blades.
G   Adequate clearance between backrest and seat to ensure free movement of buttocks.

(People adopt many sitting postures but the assessment of a good fit is the simultaneous satisfaction of the above seven criteria.)

Figure 22.1 Fit of person to chair and table
From BS 5873: Part 1

22.2 Office furniture

BS 5940 deals with the dimensions of office workstations, desks, tables and chairs. It covers definitions and measurement methods as well as dimensional recommendations. It also includes a table of anthropometric data—which differs somewhat from that given in table 3.1 of this book, since it was compiled on the basis of the limited data available at the time.

Chairs

Dimensional requirements for office chairs are given in table 22.1 and figure 22.2.

- Chairs in general should be stable throughout the full range of postures which a user is likely to adopt. (Non-rotatable chairs should conform to BS 4875:Part 1 in this respect and rotatable chairs to BS 5459:Part 2.) The standard does not make any recommendations concerning how this should be achieved but for rotatable chairs a five-point base of support is generally considered desirable.

- The seat surface should be 'substantially flat'. No part should be more than 25 mm higher than any other. The upper surface of the front edge should be resilient or rounded. 'It is recommended that the seat be padded or upholstered' (if not, it should be slightly sloped—maximum angle = 5°). Upholstery materials should be permeable to air and water vapour. 'All items should be designed and constructed, so as to reduce the hazards of ignition and of fire growth' (see BS 5852:Part 1 and BS 6336).

- 'The backrest of an office chair shall provide adequate support for the office worker in the lumbar region. It should also be shaped and dimensioned so as to leave space for the buttocks and for movements of the shoulder blades. In addition, backrests of chairs shall permit arm and elbow movement'—see comments.

Tables

- Dimensional requirements for desks, tables, worktops and drawers are given in table 22.2 and figure 22.3.

- In plan view, the length O of the desktop, table or worktop should be some multiple of 100 mm and the width P some multiple of 50 mm (see section 19 concerning the principles of modular coordination).

Preferred sizes are as follows:

Length O	Width P (see figure 22.3)
1200	600
1200	800
1600	800

Foot rests

- Dimensional requirements for foot rests are as follows:
  - Length Q_1: 450 mm minimum
  - Width Q_2: 350 mm minimum
  - Height: Fixed front edge I_1 40 + 5 mm
  - Rear edge I_2 100 mm minimum
  - Adjustable front edge I_1 35 mm minimum
  - Slope ß: 0° to 20°

Table 22.1 Dimensions of chairs   Dimensions in mm

Seat

A	Seat height: Chair with fixed height seat	440
	Chair with adjustable height seat, minimum range of adjustment	420 to 500 (see note 1)
B	Effective seat depth:	
	Chair with fixed back	380 minimum 430 maximum
	Chair with adjustable back, minimum range of adjustment	380 minimum 470 maximum
		380 to 420 (see note 1)
B_1	Seat pad depth	380 minimum
C	Seat width	400 minimum
α	Slope of the seat in relation to the horizontal	0° to 5° (see note 2)

Back

W	Vertical height of X above Z:	
	Chair with fixed backrest	210 ± 15
	Chair with adjustable backrest, minimum range of adjustment	170 minimum 250 maximum
		170 to 230 (see note 1)
V	Vertical height of area of essential lumbar support (having X at its centre)	100 minimum
F	Width of area of essential lumbar support:	
	General-purpose chair	360 minimum
	Machine operator's chair	360 minimum 400 maximum
U	Horizontal curvature of lumbar support, radius	400 minimum

Armrests (if fitted)

G	Height of armrests above point Z of the seat	200 minimum 250 maximum (see note 3)
G_1	Inside distance between armrests	460 minimum 525 maximum
G_2	Set back of armrests in relation to the front of the seat	100 minimum
G_3	Length of the armrests	200 minimum
G_4	Width of the armrests	40 minimum

Notes

1. The range of adjustment provided shall include at least the specified minimum range and may be larger.

2. Preferred angle $3 \pm 1°$.

3. Preferred height 215 mm minimum, 230 mm maximum.

From BS 5940: Part 1

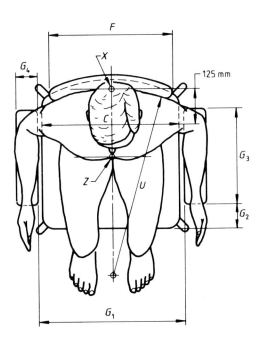

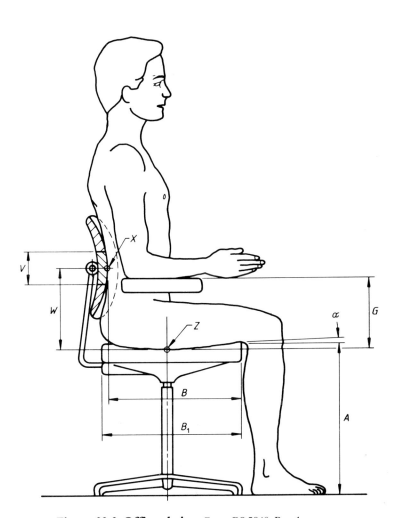

Figure 22.2 Office chairs   From BS 5940: Part 1

Table 22.2 Dimensions of desks, tables, worktops and drawers

Dimensions in mm

Desks, tables and worktops	General-purpose	Machine operator's
H Height of top surface:		
Fixed height top	720 ± 10	670 ± 10
Adjustable height top recommended adjustment range (see note 1)	670 to 770	610 to 720
Leg room		
R Clearance below desk top:		
Fixed height top	650 min.	620 min.
Adjustable height top	620 min.	580 min.
T Clearance across the kneehole	580 min.	580 min.
S Leg room, front to back	450 min.	450 min.
S_1 Leg room, front to back	600 min.	600 min.

Drawers (see note 2)	Horizontal storage	Suspended filing	Other types
Internal dimensions of usable space			
Length, front to back	420 min.	420 min.	Not defined
Width, nominal	330	330	330
Height	120 min. (see note 3)	270 min. 290 max.	Not defined

Notes.
1. If adjustment is provided in fixed steps, the steps should not exceed 30 mm.
2. Dimensioned to suit size in accordance with BS 1467 and BS 4264.
3. For horizontal storage of A4 files and vertical storage of A6 cards.

From BS 5940: Part 1

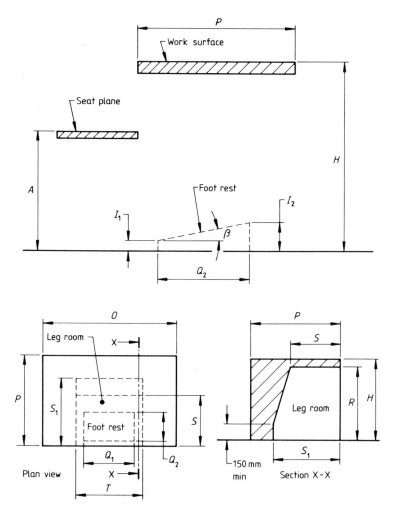

Figure 22.3 Desk, table, worktop, foot-rest and leg room
From BS 5940: Part 1

Comments

1   The working posture (and hence the comfort and well-being) of a person sitting at a writing desk will be (in part at least) determined by (a) the height of the seat and (b) the height of the desk. Let us suppose that an optimal configuration is achieved when (a) the seat height is equal to the user's popliteal height and (b) the desk is 50 mm above the user's elbow height. In order to *meet these criteria exactly*, for the 5th percentile to 95th percentile range of adult users as described in table 3.1, it may be calculated that (a) the seat height must be adjustable from 400 mm to 515 mm; and (b) the desk height must be adjustable from 670 mm to 830 mm.

In practice, lesser degrees of adjustment will be adequate since minor deviations from the 'ideal' postures are of no consequence and the criteria of an effective match are in reality 'fuzzy'. The heights quoted in the standard are something of a compromise. The 720 mm fixed height desk, used with an adjustable chair, should be reasonably satisfactory for most British adults—although the taller man will have to set his chair a little too low for comfort and the shorter person will benefit from the use of a footrest.

2   The standard does not specify either the overall height or the shape of the backrest. Traditionally, typists' chairs have had a low level backrest which supports the lumbar region and leaves the shoulders free. The latter requirement has probably been over-emphasized and the desirability of also supporting the upper part of the back is being increasingly recognized. Grandjean (1981) recommends a backrest which extends 500 mm above the level of the seat.

22.3 School furniture

The provision of a range of furniture sizes, suitable for children and young people of various ages in schools and other educational establishments, is an ergonomic problem of considerable complexity. ISO 5970 and BS 5873 both address this problem.

ISO 5970 specifies seven sizes which are numbered from 0 to 6. When BS 5873 was drafted, it was concluded that the first and last members of this series were not required to match the 3 to 18 year old population in British schools. An intermediate size, number 2.5 was, however, inserted. The dimensions of the BS 5873 range of standard sizes are given in table 22.3 together with the system of colour coding used for their identification. Additional recommendations for the dimensions of table tops for dining are given in table 22.4.

The 5½ standard sizes are specified according to the ranges of unshod statures of the children for whom they are intended. (The criteria of a good fit are given in figure 22.1.) The age ranges to which these stature ranges approximately correspond are shown in figure 22.4 (this is an appendix of the original standard which is for guidance only and does not constitute part of the standard). Hence, for a school which has pupils from 5 to 11 years of age, sizemarks 2 and 3 will be required.

Additional information—The ergonomics of seating in general and of various specific types of seating are discussed at length in Pheasant (1986) and in PP 7310.

Table 22.3 Dimensions and colour identification of school furniture

Dimensions in mm unless otherwise shown

		Sizemark	1	2	2.5 (see note 1)	3	4	5
		Colour of symbol of sizemark (see note 2)	Orange 06 E 53	Violet 22 E 53	Black 00 E 53	Yellow 10 E 53	Red 04 E 53	Green 14 E 53
		Recommended stature ranges (see note 3)	1000 to 1120	1120 to 1300	1180 to 1360	1300 to 1480	1480 to 1620	1620 and over
Seat	h_5	Height of seat (see note 4)	260 ± 3	300 ± 3	320 ± 3	340 ± 3	380 ± 3	420 ± 3
	t_4	Effective depth of seat (see note 5)	250 to 270	280 to 300		320 to 340	350 to 370	370 to 390
	b_3	Minimum width of seat	250	270		290	320	340
	b_5	Maximum width of chair (see note 6)	380	380		380	430	430
	r_1	Radius of front edge of seat (see note 7)	30 to 40	30 to 40		30 to 40	30 to 40	30 to 40
	δ	Maximum angle of seat (see note 8)	4°	4°		4°	4°	4°
Backrest	β	Angle between seat and backrest (see note 9)	95° to 100°	95° to 100°		95° to 100°	95° to 100°	95° to 100°
	h_6	Seat plane to bottom of backrest (see notes 10 and 11)	110 to 120	120 to 130		140 to 150	150 to 160	160 to 170
	h_7	Seat plane to top of backrest	210 to 250	250 to 280		280 to 310	310 to 330	330 to 360
	b_4	Minimum width of backrest	250	250		250	280	300
	r_2	Minimum radius of backrest	400	400		400	400	400
Tables	h_1	Height of top (see note 12)	460 ± 3	520 ± 3	540 ± 3	580 ± 3	640 ± 3	700 ± 3
	t_1	Minimum depth of top (see note 13)	550	550		550	550	550
	b_1	Minimum length of top, 1 place (see note 13)	550	550		550	550	550
		Minimum length of top, 2 place (see note 13)	1100	1100		1100	1100	1100
Leg clearance	b_2	Minimum width between supports, 1 place	470	470		470	470	470
		Minimum width between supports, 2 place	1000	1000		1000	1000	1000
	t_2	Minimum depth of knee zone	300	300		300	350	400
	t_3	Minimum depth of tibia zone	400	400		400	450	500
	h_2	Minimum height of knee zone	400	460		520	580	640
	h_4	Minimum height of tibia zone	250	250		300	300	350

Table 22.3 *(continued)*

Notes.

1. If sizemark 2.5 chairs and tables are used, it is recommended that sizemark 2 chairs be reduced in seat height to 290 ± 3 mm and sizemark 2 tables be reduced in table top height to 510 ± 3 mm, the other dimensions remaining as given for sizemark 2. Except for seat and table top heights, sizemarks 2 and 2.5 have identical dimensions.

2. *Colour symbol of sizemark.* The code numbers specified are from BS 5252.

3. *Recommended stature ranges.* See figure 22.4.

4. *Height of seat (h_5).* The height of the seat is measured to the highest point at the front of the seating area on the centre line.

5. *Effective seat depth (t_4).* The effective seat depth is measured on the centre line of the seat plane from the front edge to a perpendicular line from h_6. The back edge of the seat may have a radius in plan, but not less than r_2 (400 mm).

6. *Maximum width of chair (b_5).* The maximum width of chair applies to the forward part of the seat or frame which may in use project under the table.

7. *Radius of front edge of seat (r_1).* This is an approximate specification of the top surface.

8. *Maximum angle of seat plane (δ).* The main part of the seating surface has to lie between the horizontal and maximum slope of 4°. The seating surface may be flat or include dishing. Any dishing has not to exceed 10 mm in depth and has to occur in the back ⅔ of the effective seat depth. The deepest part of the dishing has to occur ¾ of the effective seat depth back from the front edge.

9. *Angle between seat and backrest planes (β).* The angle between the seat and backrest planes is measured on the centre line of the seat. For chairs of sizemarks 4 and 5 designed for extended periods of sitting, i.e. in lecture and assembly halls, angle β may be increased up to a maximum of 106°.

10. *Seat plane to bottom of backrest (h_6).* This defines the foremost point of the backrest. It complies with and substitutes for W in ISO 5970.

11. *Lower and upper limits of backrest (h_6 and h_7).* The lower and upper limits of the backrest are measured on the centre line of the seat plane from the lowest part of the seating surface. The upper and lower edges of the backrest have to be well rounded.

12. *Height of top (h_1).* Table top surfaces are horizontal. When an inclined surface is required, an inclination of 16° is recommended. The edge towards the pupil has to be approximately at the same height as the specified horizontal surface.

13. *Depth and length of table tops (t_1 and b_1).* The dimensions specified allow for pupils to sit at the ends and sides of tables. The dimensions of table tops intended only for 1 or 2 pupils at one side are specified in ISO 5970 and are as given below; the table tops exclusively for this purpose should conform to these dimensions.

Sizemark	1	2	3	4	5
	mm	mm	mm	mm	mm
t_1	450	500	500	500	500
b_1 (one place)	600	600	700	700	700
b_1 (two place)	1200	1200	1300	1300	1300

Other table plan sizes should conform to the following increments:

　t_1　450 mm to 1200 mm: 50 mm increments

　b_1　450 mm to 800 mm: 50 mm increments

　b_1　800 mm to 2000 mm: 100 mm increments

From BS 5873: Part 1

Table 22.4 Dimensions of table tops for dining

Furniture sizemark	Minimum table area per place, m² (see note 1)	Minimum table perimeter per place, mm (see notes 1 and 2)	
		Rectangular tables	Other shapes
1	0.15	480	480
2 to 5 inclusive	0.15	550	480

Note 1. The relationship between area and perimeter varies with the shape of the table. It is important to ensure that both the minimum criteria are met.

Note 2. These dimensions govern the minimum permissible perimeter to the table. Lengths of straight sides need not necessarily be multiples of 480 mm or 550 mm.

From BS 5873: Part 1

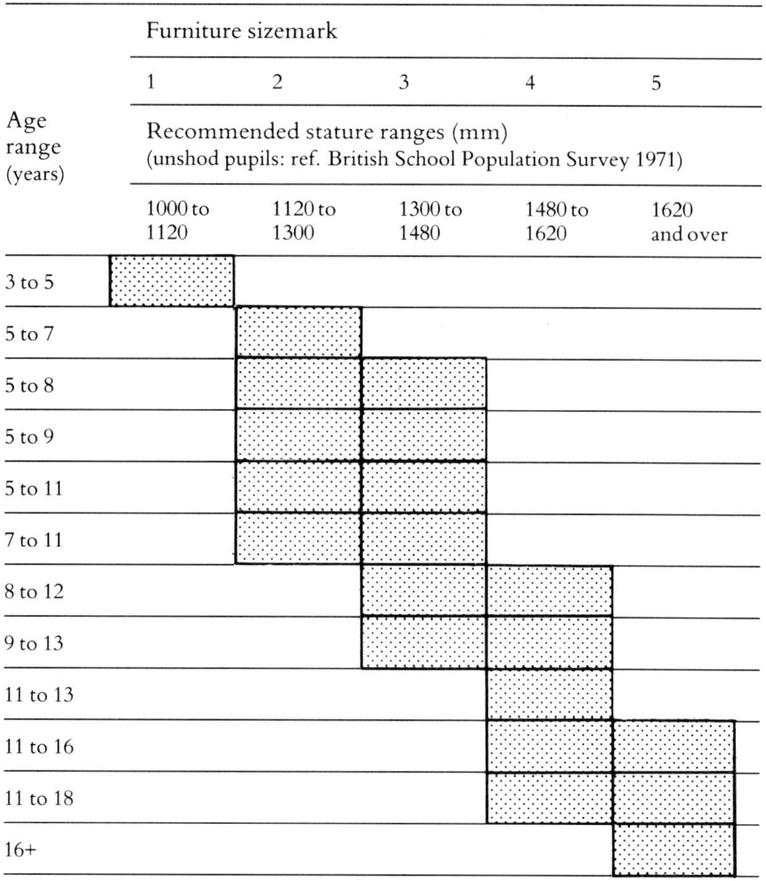

Age range (years)	Furniture sizemark				
	1	2	3	4	5
	Recommended stature ranges (mm) (unshod pupils: ref. British School Population Survey 1971)				
	1000 to 1120	1120 to 1300	1300 to 1480	1480 to 1620	1620 and over
3 to 5	▨				
5 to 7		▨			
5 to 8		▨	▨		
5 to 9		▨	▨		
5 to 11		▨	▨		
7 to 11		▨			
8 to 12			▨	▨	
9 to 13			▨	▨	
11 to 13				▨	
11 to 16				▨	▨
11 to 18				▨	▨
16+					▨

Note Sizemark 2.5 has been included in this standard to meet specifically the 7 to 9 years age range. When sizemark 2.5 is used for the 5 to 7 years age range, sizemark 2 seat and table top heights should be reduced to 290 mm and 510 mm respectively (see note 1 to table 22.3).

Figure 22.4 Distribution of school furniture sizes
From BS 5873: Part 1

Section 23 Kitchen equipment

The following section pertains to domestic kitchens—rather than those which serve public buildings, commercial premises, etc.

In designing a kitchen, or specifying the dimensions of kitchen equipment, two main sets of requirements must be considered:

1 the ergonomic and functional requirements of the users;
2 the dimensional (modular) coordination of products.

The principal British and International Standards which deal with these matters are BS 1195, BS 3705, BS 6222, ISO 3055, ISO 5731, ISO 5732. Sinks are dealt with in BS 1244.

These standards define the dimensions of a coordinated range of sizes of kitchen units of three principal types (as shown in figure 23.1).

1 the *base unit* which is fitted with (or able to support) a worktop and generally stands upon the floor;
2 the *wall unit* which is hung on the wall, generally above a base unit;
3 the *tall unit* which normally stands on the floor and is equal in height to the top of a wall unit.

These may be modified to house sinks or appliances. (The latter may also be free standing.)

Specifications for the coordinating dimensions of kitchen equipment as given in BS 6222 and ISO 3055, are presented in table 23.1.

Note that in table 23.1 and in the discussion which follows, the length of a unit refers to its dimension in plan measured from side to side (i.e. parallel to the wall against which it stands), and the breadth of a unit is its dimension from front to back (i.e. perpendicular to the wall). This follows the usage of BS 6222 and

ISO 5731 but differs from that of ISO 3055.

Worktop heights

BS 3705 (published in 1972) contains the following statement: 'Subject to the need for field research and solving technical problems, it is thought that a 50 mm incremental range of heights of working surfaces may be adopted in the future, the ranges being 900 mm to 1050 mm for sinks and 850 mm to 1050 mm for worktops. Because studies show that generally the worktop surface needs to be higher than the present 850 mm worktop height, for the greater number of users, this standard is omitting the 850 mm although this might be included in any subsequent range after the above work is completed. As an interim measure, the standard will remain at BS 3705 (imperial) height rounded off metrically to 900 mm for sinks and worktops.'

However, BS 6222: Part 1 (published in 1982) reads as follows: 'The coordinating heights of all units and appliances shall be as follows:

(a) Top of worktop: either 900 mm or 850 mm (second preference)'.

An annex to ISO 3055 (which does not constitute part of the standard) contains the following:

'The appropriate working heights for different activities when standing are
— for food preparation: 850 mm to 1000 mm;
— for washing up: 900 mm to 1050 mm.

A worktop level of 850 mm and 900 mm is specified in 4.1.* 'To make allowance for differing statures and activities, a range, at intervals of 50 mm, up to 1050 mm is desirable. Adjustments in height can be different plinth heights and other means'.

* This refers to a clause in ISO 3055:1985

Table 23.1 Coordinating dimensions for kitchen equipment

Dimensions in mm

	BS 6222	ISO 3055	Notes
Length (along wall)			
Cabinets		300, 400, 500, 600, 800	1
Base units and wall units	300, 400, 500, 600, 1000, 1200		
Tall units	500, 600		
Sink units	1000, 1200, 1500, 1800	600, 800, 900, 1200, 1500, 1800	
Appliance housing units	600		
Appliances	600	600	
Width (front to back)			
Worktop, base unit, sink unit, tall unit	600 or 500 (2nd preference)	600	
Wall unit	300	300 or 350	
Height (from floor)			
Top of worktop	900 or 850 (second preferred)	900 or 850	2
Underside of wall unit	1300	$1300 \text{ minimum} + n \times 100$	3,4
Top of wall unit or tall unit	1950 minimum	$1900 \text{ minimum} + n \times 100$	
	2250 maximum	(2100 preferred)	
Toe recess			
Height	150 (for 900 mm worktop)	150 (for 900 mm worktop)	5
	100 (for 850 mm worktop)	100 (for 850 mm worktop)	
Depth	50	50	
Thickness of worktop	30	30	

Notes.
1. ISO 3055 specifies that the length of all components shall be multiples of the standard module M (where M = 100 mm). The figures given in the table are quoted as *preferred* sizes.
2. See also subsequent discussion.
3. The zone required for lighting shall be included in the wall unit space.
4. *n* is an integer.
5. In ISO 3055 this dimension is referred to as the plinth height.

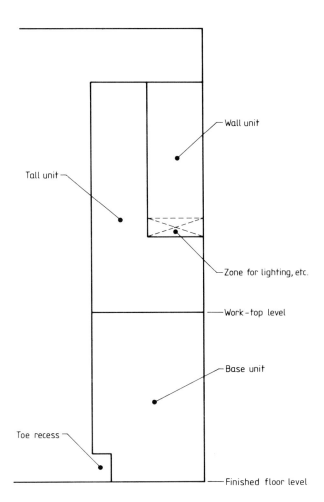

Figure 23.1 Coordinated kitchen units   From BS 6222: Part 1

Labels on figure:
- Wall unit
- Tall unit
- Zone for lighting, etc.
- Work-top level
- Base unit
- Toe recess
- Finished floor level

Comments—The above statements have been quoted at length, since they pertain to important ergonomic issues which have been the subject of extensive research. (An introduction to this research literature will be found in Pheasant, (1986).)

The problem may be summarized as follows:

1 People of different sizes, performing the same task, require different worktop heights;

2 A particular person requires different worktop heights when performing different tasks.

The range of heights suggested in BS 3705 and in the annex to ISO 3055 (850 mm to 1050 mm) should satisfactorily accommodate most of the user population, performing typical food preparation tasks. (But the logistic problems of matching worktops to users may well be considerable—especially in households where users of widely different statures share a kitchen.) It also makes good ergonomic sense for the rim of the sink to be higher than the level of the main worktop (in order to equalize the height at which work in actually performed)—although the locations at which the changes of level occur have to be chosen with care so as not to break the flow of activities. It is particularly important that level changes should not occur in the vicinity of the hob, where they could be hazardous; and it may well be undesirable for the hob itself to be higher than the 900 mm which is customary at present.

(The idea of level changes has not proved popular among architects and designers.)

There is little doubt that a uniform standard height of 900 mm is uncomfortably low for a sizeable proportion of the user population (and 850 mm is of course worse). However, it must be pointed out that, even for a tall person, a relatively low worktop may be desirable for some activities—rolling pastry for example. But since these activities represent a relatively small proportion of kitchen work they should not be allowed to determine the main worktop height. One solution to this problem may be the provision of a low-level accessory worktop—perhaps one that can be pulled out from the main units. If this is 750 mm high it will also be suitable for seated use with conventional upright chairs (for eating, writing, etc.).

The 900 mm standard height for worktops, base units and sinks was described in BS 3705 as an 'interim measure'. It has subsequently acquired an air of permanence. Ergonomically this is undesirable.

Kitchen layout

BS 3705 includes the following recommendations:

- The sequence of work surface/cooker or hob unit/work surface/sink/work surface is of first importance. This may be equally well laid out in a straight line, a U-shape or an L provided that the sequence is not broken by a door or other traffic way.

- It is undesirable for the sink and cooker or hob unit to be on opposite walls, particularly if there would be a through passage between them.

- For safety reasons, the cooker or hob unit should never be under a window nor should it be next to a passageway or in a corner.

- The floors of a kitchen and dining area and any passage between should be at the same level.

Comment—For right handed users (who comprise approximately 90% of the population) it is more natural for the sink to be at the left of the cooker or hob. For further discussion see Pheasant (1986).

Figure 23.2 is taken from an annex to ISO 3055. It shows the recommended sizes of kitchen fittings as a function of household size.

Miscellaneous recommendations
(from ISO 3055 Annex B which does not form part of the standard)

- *Vertical reach* A convenient range of vertical reach for the storage of frequently used items is 400 to 1800 mm from the floor. Refrigerators and freezers should be located within this zone. (For wheelchair users this is generally limited to 1200 mm.)

- For convenient loading the top of a dishwasher should not be more than 1100 mm above the floor.

- Ovens should be located so that the setting down surface (such as the door face or tray) is level with the adjacent worktop or pull-out working surface.

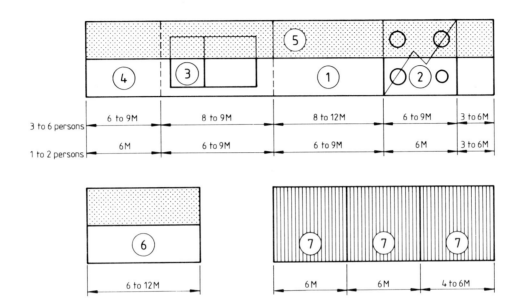

Key to figure 23.2.

M is the basic module of 100 mm.

1 Main worktop—if a low level pull-out worktop is provided it should be located next to the sink; it should be 6 M from side to side and 4 M from front to back.
2 Cooker—a heat resistant setting down area, at least 3 M in length, should be provided adjacent to the cooker.
3 Sink bowl unit.
4 Sink top unit for clean dishes.

5 Wall units—wide hinge-doors opening over the working area are disadvantageous.
6 Additional worktop—at least 6 M if used just for setting down or 8 M if used for working purposes.
7 Tall units to include the refrigerator/freezer, additional shelf space, etc. The number of refrigerator and freezer units 'depends more on the way of life than on the number of persons in the household'.

Figure 23.2 Kitchen space and equipment requirements
From ISO 3055

Activity space requirements

The following recommendations are quoted from an annex to
ISO 3055 (which is not part of the standard). See also sections 20
and 21.

|_600_| |_800_|

One person passing between a wall and
piece of furniture or between furniture.

|_900_| |_900_|

One person carrying cleaning equipment or
two persons in places with light traffic only.

Space for movement Dimensions in mm

|_1200_|

Width of main circulation routes.

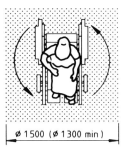

| ∅ 1500 (∅ 1300 min) |

Turning space for wheelchairs.
The specified area can in some
cases be reduced if there is free
space under a piece of furniture
or equipment.

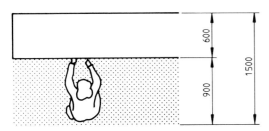

Taking something out of a floor unit (except a low-level oven) or a tall unit.

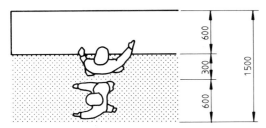

One person working, another passing.

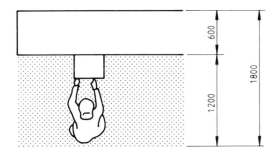

Taking cooking out of a low-level oven.

Equipment/user zone

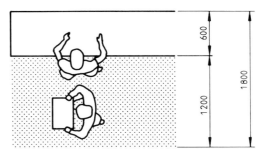

One person working, another passing with a tray.

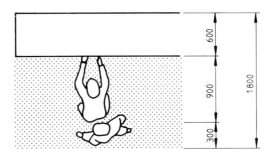

One person taking something out of floor unit, another passing sideways.

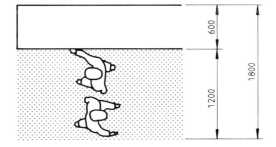

Two people passing.

It should be noted that the distance between a row of units and a parallel wall or row of units oposite should be at least 12M. For wheelchair users, 14M is preferable.

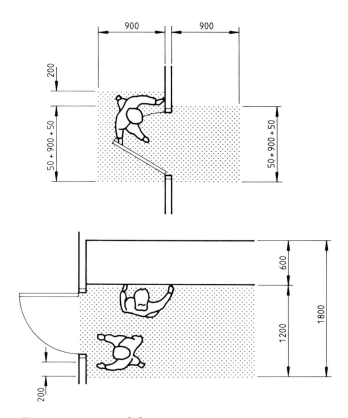

Free space around door Dimensions in mm

Free space on each side of doors with a doorset width of 9M.

Inner face:
50 mm + 900 mm + 50 mm + 200 mm (latch side)
Depth 900 mm

Outer face:
50 mm + 900 mm + 50 mm
Depth 900 mm

Needs of turning wheelchairs can dictate the size of the free space around doors.

Outward-opening door:
200 mm to equipment on the latch side.

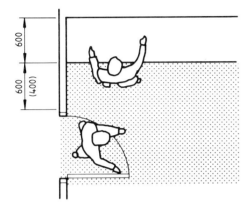

Inward-opening door:
400 mm for standing working.

Hinged doors not more than 4M wide:
600 mm for wider doors or appliances.

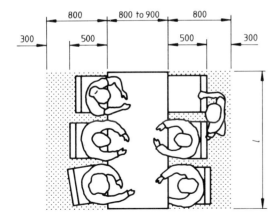

Dimensions in mm

Eating/equipment

A dining table should be at least 800 mm wide with 800 mm of unobstructed space on both sides for chairs and access.

Values of l:

Number of persons (n)	l
2	800 mm
4	1 200 mm
6	1 800 mm
8	2 400 ($n \times 600$) mm

Section 24 Safeguarding machinery

The safeguarding of potentially hazardous machinery commonly requires the provision of a barrier which will prevent the user from reaching into the danger area.

Figure 24.1 is taken from BS 5304 which deals specifically with the *mechanical* hazards of machinery—that is, those which are in some way associated with its moving parts. (The standard does not apply to electrical, thermal, chemical or other non-mechanical hazards.)

Figure 24.1 deals with situations in which it is necessary to provide a slotted opening in the guard of a machine, for the purpose of feeding in or removing material. It must not be possible for the user's fingers to reach the dangerous moving parts of the machine (or hazard point). The greater the depth (A) of the slot (i.e. its lesser dimension) the greater must be the distance (B) between the guard and the hazard point. For example, if it is necessary to

provide a slot which is 55 mm deep, then the guard should be at least 450 mm from the hazards. (Note that the width of the slot is not relevant.)

BS 3042 specifies the constructional details and methods of use of a number of standardized probing devices for checking protection against mechanical, electrical and thermal hazards. Figure 24.2 shows one of these—a device known as *test finger IV* which is intended to meet the standard of protection implied by the recommendations of BS 5304.

Note—See BS 3402 for constructional details of test finger IV and for information concerning other similiar devices.

DIN 31 001 Part 1 provides an alternative and more comprehensive set of data concerning *safety distances* required between barriers or guards and hazard points. Figures for adults and young people over 14 and for adults and children over 3 are included; only the former will be given here. The dimensions given are deemed to 'represent

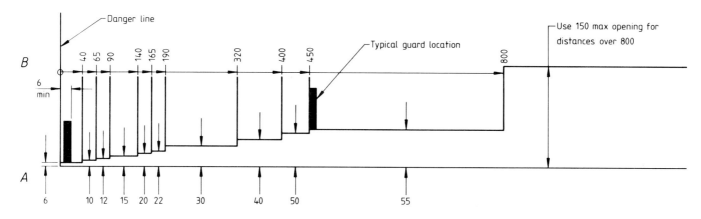

Figure 24.1 Openings in fixed guards   From BS 5304   Dimensions in mm

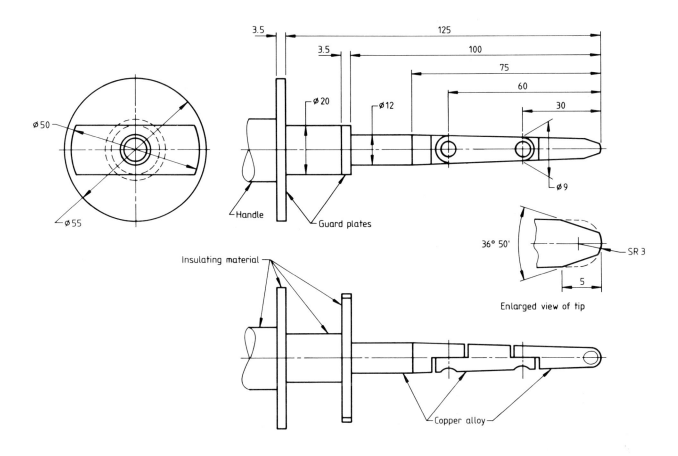

Dimensions in mm
Note. The size of the handle is immaterial
Figure 24.2 Test finger IV   From BS 3042

a compromise between safety, economic practicability and ease of application'.

Figure 24.3 and table 24.1 show safety distances when *reaching over* an obstacle such as a barrier or the edge of a machine.

  a = distance of a hazard point from floor
  b = height of edge of safety device
  c = horizontal distance of edge from hazard point

Comment—These figures have received a certain amount of criticism. A few adult males are able to reach further and would therefore be at risk (Thompson and Booth 1982). The highest level quoted is 2400 mm, since the standard considers the safety distance for overhead reaching to be 2500 mm—again this is risky (Pheasant 1986).

Figure 24.4 shows the radius of movement of parts of the body reaching around a fixed edge. It is assumed that any further advance of the limb towards the hazard point is prevented in some way.

Comment—The figure of 850 mm for the whole upper limb can probably be exceeded by a small proportion (approx 2%) of British adult men.

Figure 24.5 shows safety distances for the action of reaching through rectangular, square or circular openings.

Figure 24.6 deals with safety distances at *squeeze points*; that is, those situations in which there is a danger of the body (or part of it) being trapped between moving parts.

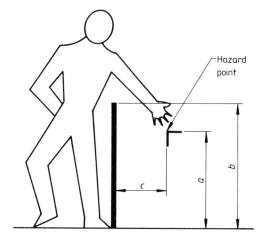

Figure 24.3 Hazard point reaching down or over   From DIN 31 001 Part 1

Table 24.1 Safety distances from hazard point   Dimensions in mm

| Distance of hazard point from floor a | Height of edge of safety device b | | | | | | | |
| | 2400 | 2200 | 2000 | 1800 | 1600 | 1400 | 1200 | 1000 |
	Horizontal distance c from hazard point							
2400	—	100	100	100	100	100	100	100
2200	—	250	350	400	500	500	600	600
2000	—	—	350	500	600	700	900	1100
1800	—	—	—	600	900	900	1000	1100
1600	—	—	—	500	900	900	1000	1300
1400	—	—	—	100	800	900	1000	1300
1200	—	—	—	—	500	900	1000	1400
1000	—	—	—	—	300	900	1000	1400
800	—	—	—	—	—	600	900	1300
600	—	—	—	—	—	—	500	1200
400	—	—	—	—	—	—	300	1200
200	—	—	—	—	—	—	200	1100

Values for edge b under 1000 mm have not been included because the reach does not increase any further and in addition there is the risk of falling into the hazard area.

From DIN 31 001 Part 1

Part of the body	Safety distance r	Illustration
Hand from root of finger to fingertip	≥ 120	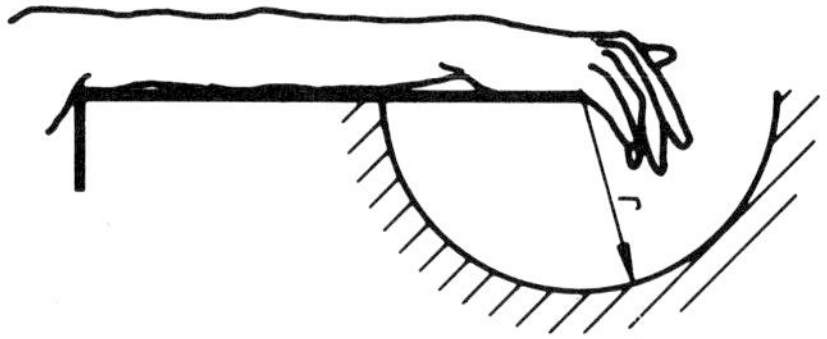
Hand from wrist to fingertip	≥ 230	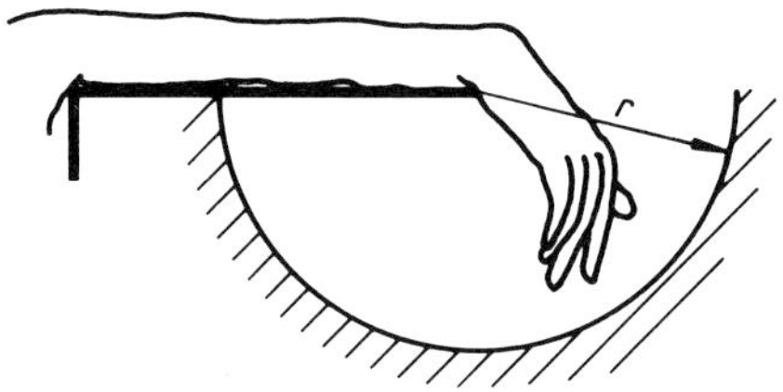
Arm from elbow to fingertip	≥ 550	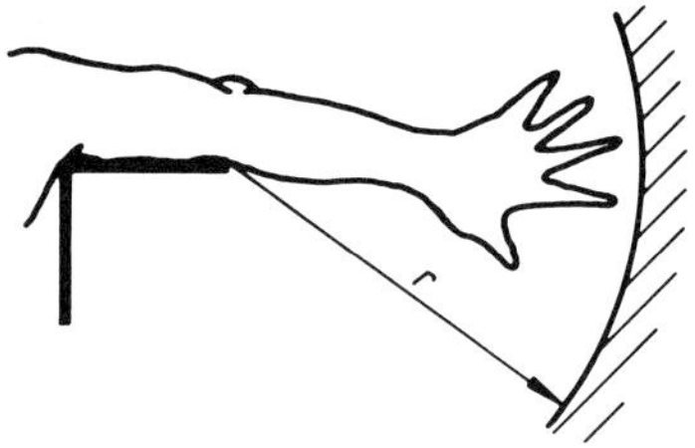
Arm from armpit to fingertip	≥ 850	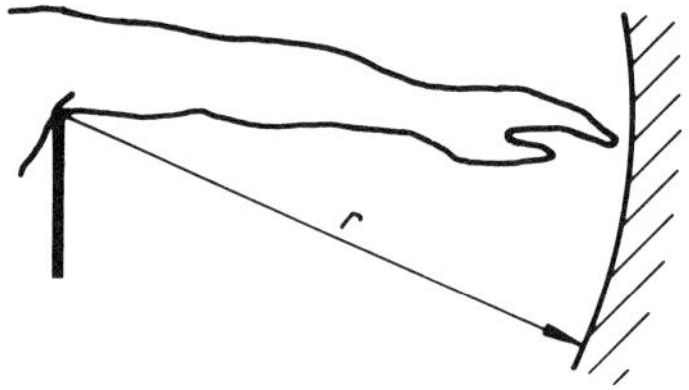

Figure 24.4 Reaching round From DIN 31 001 Part 1

Dimensions in mm

Part of the body	Fingertip	Finger		Hand to ball of thumb	Arm	—
Illustration		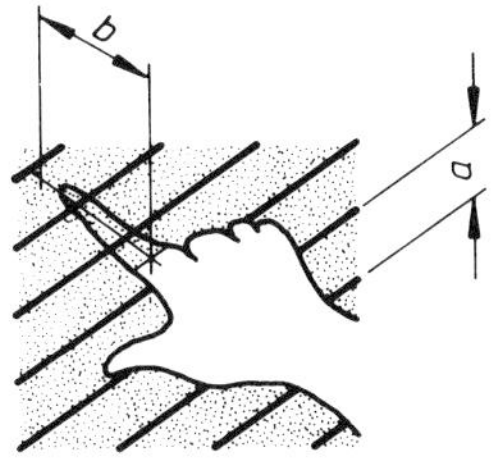		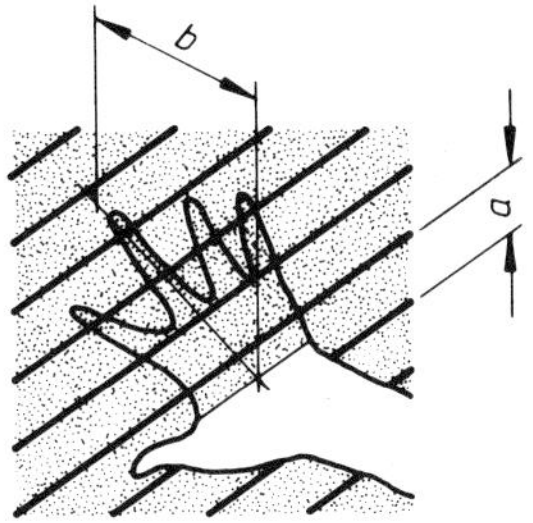	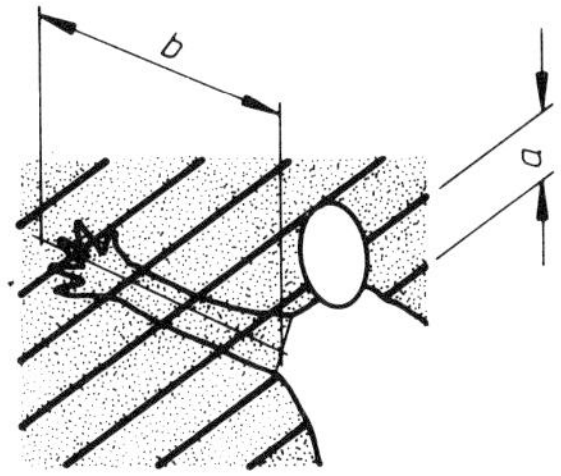	
Width of opening: rectangle or gap a	>4;≤8	>8;≤12	>12; ≤20	>20;≤30	>30;≤ 135;	>135*
Safety distance to hazard point b	≥15	≥80	≥120	≥200	≥850	—

Part of the body	Fingertip	Finger		Hand to thumb root	Arm	—
Illustration		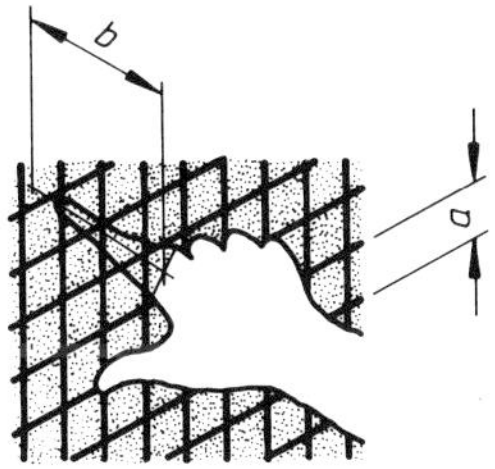		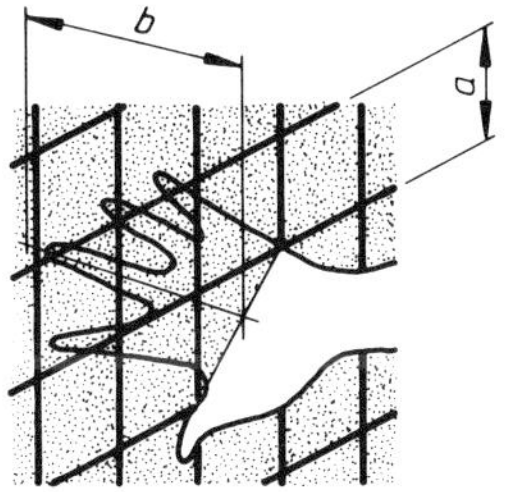	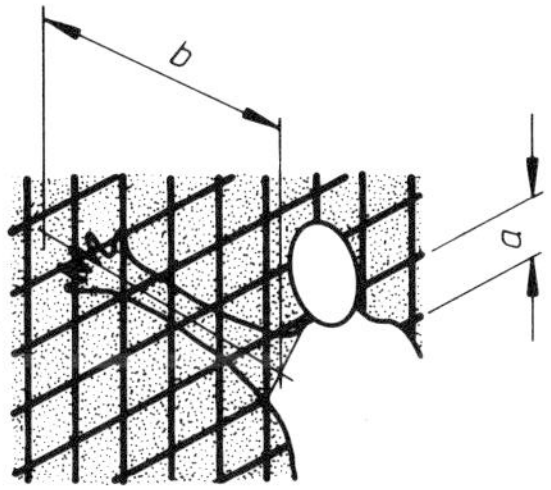	
Width of opening: diameter or length of side a	>4;≤8	>8;≤12	>12;≤25	>25;≤40	>40;≤250	>250*
Safety distance to hazard point b	≥15	≥80	≥120	≥200	≥850	—

* If dimensions exceed the stated opening width, it is possible for the body to bend over into the opening; it will thus be necessary to take into account the safety distances given in table 24.1.

Figure 24.5 Reaching into and reaching through From DIN 31 001 Part 1   Dimensions in mm

A squeeze point is not regarded as a hazard point for the parts of the body indicated if the safety distances are not less than those shown below and if it is ensured that the next largest part of the body cannot be introduced.

Part of the body	Body	Leg	Foot	Arm	Hand, wrist, fist	Finger
Safety distance	500	180	120		100	25
Illustration			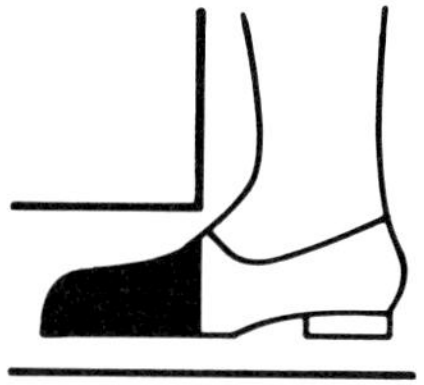			

Figure 24.6 Safety distances for adults and children at squeeze points From DIN 31 001 Part 1   Dimensions in mm

Section 25 Products for infants and children

A considerable number of British Standards deal with the safety of products which are 'used' by infants and children. A selection of these will be discussed with emphasis on the ergonomic and anthropometric issues involved. (It must be emphasized that in all cases the original standards contain numerous requirements in addition to those given below.)

Babies' dummies

BS 5239 specifies requirements for materials, construction and performance tests for babies' dummies. The parts of a dummy are shown in figure 25.1a.

Requirements of the standard include the following:

- The length of the dummy in front of the flange shall be checked using the teat penetration gauge shown in figure 25.1b. The teat shall not touch the base of the gauge.

- If the flange is circular, or of circular derivation (e.g. polygonal), the outside diameter (or circumscribing circle) should not be less than 30 mm. Minimum dimensions for non-circular flanges are shown in figure 25.1c.

- Ring dimensions are shown in figure 25.1d. The width of the ring shall be a minimum of 25 mm and, where flexible materials are used, a maximum of 45 mm. The length of the ring shall not be greater than the width. The ring shall permit the passage of a 14 mm test rod. The ring should pivot or flex, through an arc of not less than 160°, so as to touch the flange on either side.

- The knob, behind the rear face of the flange, shall be a minimum of 14 mm in length. When made from an inflexible material it shall not protrude more 17 mm. When made of a flexible

material it shall not touch the base of the teat penetration gauge.

The standard also includes detailed tests for toxicity and mechanical strength, and specifications concerning packaging.

Child safety barriers

BS 4125 is concerned with safety barriers for use in the home. It is intended that these barriers shall be fitted across openings (such as flights of stairs) in order to prevent access by children of less than 24 months of age; but they will be removable by older people able to operate the locking mechanism. Requirements include the following:

- The minimum height of the barrier above the floor shall be 750 mm. There shall be no footholds allowing children to climb. The space between the bottom rail and the floor (or between the bottom rail and a part of the barrier in contact with the floor) shall not exceed 50 mm.

- When the barrier has vertical filling bars or slats, the spacings between adjacent members shall not be more than 85 mm and not less than 60 mm. If the barrier has a mesh or lattice construction, the spacing between adjacent members shall not exceed 25 mm. Diamond mesh constructions are excluded by the standard.

- The barrier shall be adjustable in width. Instructions shall include the maximum and minimum widths of opening for which the barrier is intended. When fitted to an opening, which has the maximum width of the intended range, the gap between the vertical edge of the barrier and the edge of the opening shall not exceed 85 mm.

- The standard also includes requirements for materials, locking mechanisms, testing for strength and anchorage, instructions, packaging, etc.

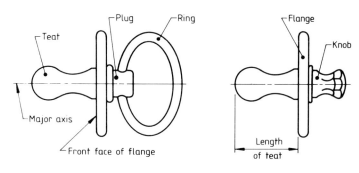

(a) Designation of features

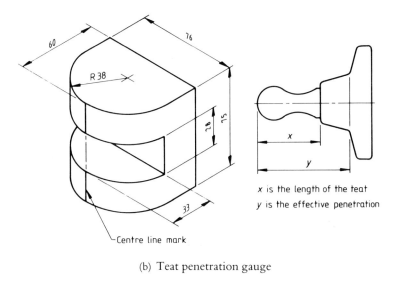

(b) Teat penetration gauge

x is the length of the teat
y is the effective penetration

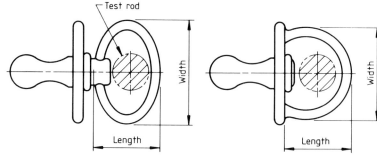

(c) Minimum dimensions of contoured, non-circular flanges

(d) Ring dimension nomenclature

Figure 25.1 Babies' dummies From BS 5239 Dimensions in mm

Cots

BS 1753 is concerned with children's cots having a mattress base length not less than 900 mm or more than 1400 mm and a width of not less than 450 mm or more than 750 mm. Mattresses for children's cots are covered by BS 1877 (Part 10) which specifies the following standard sizes:

Small cot mattress	1130 mm × 540 mm
Medium cot mattress (preferred size)	1180 mm × 550 mm
Large cot mattress	1380 mm × 680 mm

The foreword to BS 1753 draws attention to the risk of a child slipping feet first between the bars of the side of the cot and being trapped by his head. The first of the specifications which follow was drawn up with this risk in mind.

It includes the following requirements:

- The spacing, measured at any point, between adjacent members (i.e. filling bars, panels, mainframe, etc.) in the sides or ends of the cot shall not be less than 25 mm and not more than 60 mm.

- The minimum distance between the mattress base and the top edge of the sides and ends of the cot shall not be less than 595 mm. There shall be no footholds less than 510 mm above the mattress base.

- If a mattress is sold as part of the cot it shall be not more than 50 mm shorter or narrower than the internal length and width of the cot. The mattress should not reduce the internal depth of the cot to less than 495 mm.

- The standard also covers materials, deflection of parts under loading, construction, fastening devices, toys and decorative effects, packaging, instructions, etc. It also includes tests for impact, durability, stability and soluble metals.

Playpens

BS 4863 concerns rigid sided playpens for infants up to about two years old. It includes the following requirements:

- The playpen shall not be less than 600 mm high from its floor to the top of the rail that surmounts its barred sides.

- All bars or slats shall be vertical and no vertical open space shall be more than 100 mm or less than 75 mm wide.

- There shall be no intermediate horizontal bars between the top and bottom rails.

- The standard also covers other structural features, stability, strength, flammability, etc.

Fireguards

BS 6539 deals with guards for coal or wood burning appliances such as open fires, grates, room heaters and stoves. It is assumed they will be at, or within 100 mm of, floor level (as required by the Building Regulations). It is intended to protect people (especially children and the infirm) from the risks of falling into the fire, of burning themselves, or igniting their clothes. Guards of this kind are not intended to reduce the risk of fires caused by flying particles (although they may do so to some extent). The standard includes the following specifications:

- The total projected area of solid material should not exceed 20 % of the area of the complete guard (so as not to affect excessively the radiant heat of the fire).

- The aperture of mesh shall not be greater than 26 mm wide nor greater than 56 mm high. No open area shall exceed 1500 mm².

- The guard shall not be less than 650 mm high, 900 mm in width nor 400 mm in depth.

- The manufacturer must provide instructions for fixing: the guard shall not be placed closer than 300 mm to any exposed burning fuel.
- The standard also includes specifications concerning finish, strength, marking and instructions, etc.

Standards dealing with closely related products include:

BS 1945 *Fireguards for heating appliances (gas, electric and oil-burning)*
BS 3248 *Sparkguards for use with solid fuel appliances*
BS 6778 *Fireguards for use with portable free-standing or wall-mounted heating appliances*

Toys

BS 5665 also has the status of a European Standard (EN 71). It is anticipated that it will eventually form the basis of an EEC directive which will lead to a revision of the current UK regulations, The Toy (Safety) Regulations 1974 (SI 1367) which refer to an earlier standard (BS 3443). However, the edition of EN 71 upon which BS 5665 was based has been revised; and a revision of the latter standard is in progress.

BS 5665 applies to toys for children. It is considered that 14 years of age defines the end of childhood. It includes certain specific requirements concerning toys for children under 36 months.

General requirements are:

- Toys having hinged parts (such as doors or lids)—there should be a space 'between the assembled edges' which is less than 5 mm or more than 12 mm in all positions.

  Wheeled toys for riding upon (such as tricycles, scooters, cars, etc.)—there should be a space of less than 5 mm or more than 12 mm between the wheels and other parts (such as mudguards, etc.).

  Toys having winder keys or starter handles—there should be a clear space of less than 2 mm or more than 12 mm between the key

or handle and the body of the toy.

(These three requirements are presumably intended for the avoidance of finger traps—although the standard does not make this explicit.)

- Toys intended for children under 36 months
  The largest dimensions of the toy itself, or of any detachable component, should be less than 17 mm or more than 32 mm.

(These dimensions presumably are considered to define the sizes of objects which are small enough to be swallowed and large enough to be hazardous if this occurs: the standard does not however make these considerations explicit.)

The new edition of EN 71 deals with this matter differently and requires the use of a special testing device.

- Attached components which are made of non-pliable materials must either be:
  —embedded in such a way that they cannot be pulled out by a child's fingers or teeth, or;
  —fixed in such a way that they cannot be detached or loosened if submitted to a force of 50 N if the largest accessible dimension is less than or equal to 6 mm; or a force of 90 N when the largest accessible dimension is greater than 6 mm. (Note that the latter requirements differ slightly from those of the 1974 UK regulations.)

A variety of other mechanical and physical properties are covered by Part 1 of the standard. Part 2 deals with flammability.

Outdoor play equipment

BS 5696 deals with the design, testing, installation and maintenance of children's play equipment (such as swings, roundabouts, slides, etc.) intended for permanent installation outdoors.

Part 2 includes the following specifications:

- *Access* Several means of fixed access to the top of items such as slides are discussed. Ramps should not be used at angles in excess of 38°; at angles 15°–38° they should have footholds. A variety of steps, stairs and ladders, for use at angles greater than 15°, is described in detail.

- *Protective rails* are required to all equipment other than climbing frames with access more than 500 mm above the ground or adjacent surfaces. Handrails for steps, stairs, etc. should be between 500 mm and 900 mm above a given step in a flight (measured in a vertical line tangential to the nosing of the next step up). The minimum acceptable height for the guard rail to a platform (or a ramp) is 0.5 m when the platform is 1 m above the ground; rising linearly to 0.9 m when the platform is 1.5 m above the ground and remaining constant thereafter. The space below guard rails shall be filled in. If the infilling material is perforated it shall not have holes greater than 25 mm in any direction. If vertical bars are used they shall not be separated by more than 100 mm. The infilling shall not form traps (see below).

- *Clearance and traps* Part 1 of the standard describes a method of test for finger, hand, limb and head traps. The method, which uses test probes as shown in figure 25.2a, is summarized in figure 25.2b.

Part 2 of the standard defines a wedge trap as one which is formed by an acute angle between two or more adjacent parts that converge in a downward direction. It requires that there shall be none of these in accessible areas 1 m or more above the ground.

Part 2 of the standard also includes detailed recommendations concerning agility equipment, slides, swings, rockers, roundabouts, etc. Part 3 is a code of practice for installation and maintenance.

Other products

Numerous other products are covered by British Standards which deal with the safety of infants and children. These include:

—Child safety seats and harnesses	BS 3254
—Carry cot restraints	BS AU 186
—Seat belt booster cushions	BS AU 185
—Carry cots	BS 3881
—Baby walkers	BS 4648
—Prams	BS 4139
—Pushchairs	BS 4792
—Safety harnesses	BS 3785
—Sleepwear	BS 5722
—High chairs	BS 5799
—Protective hats for horse and pony riders	BS 6473
—Packagings resistant to opening by children	BS 6652
—Baby nests	BS 6595

These are briefly reviewed in the British Standard publication PP 1550 *Playing safe with British Standards* which is an illustrated guide for parents.

Comment—The standards cited in this section contain a considerable amount of ergonomic information concerning the safety of infants and children. It has not been possible to check all these recommendations against independent sources. At present this information exists only in the form of recommendations for specific products. More general guidelines would also be desirable concerning safety distances, barriers heights, finger traps, head traps, etc. In some cases these will need to be separately established for different age groups. Much of the necessary data already exists but the task of checking and cross-referencing between sources would be considerable.

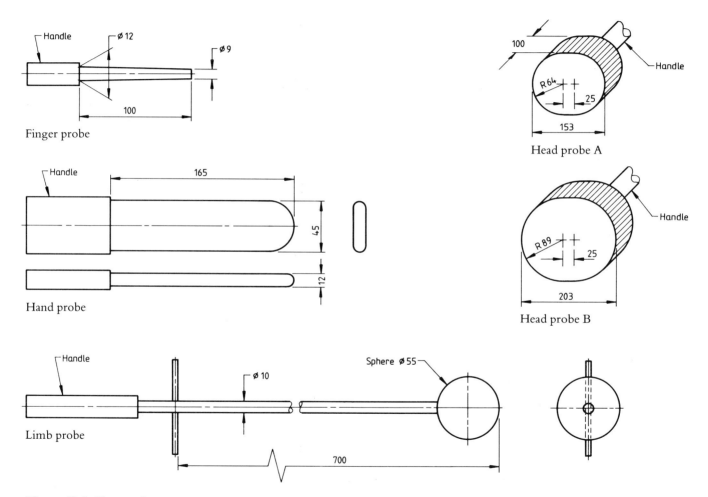

Figure 25.2a Test probes   From BS 5696: Part 1   All dimensions in mm

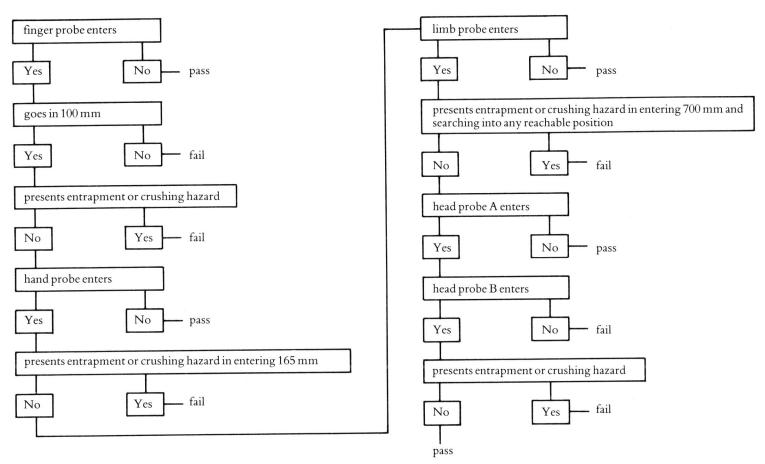

Figure 25.2b Chart showing openings which pass or fail probe tests   From BS 5696: Part 1

Section 26 Controls

The following general remarks apply to devices, such as push buttons, switches, levers and pedals, by means of which a person controls the operation of a machine.

26.1 General

Identification and coding

In most ordinary applications it will be sufficient to *identify* a control by means of a label (either verbal or symbolic—see sections 16 and 17). In special cases (e.g. for critical operations or where controls are numerous) it may be appropriate to assist the operator by some additional form of *coding* e.g. size, shape or colour.

Where a control must be operated 'blind' it should be shape coded (i.e. identifiable by touch alone) and separated from adjacent controls by 125 mm (MIL-STD-1472C).

Colour coding of push buttons is discussed in section 17.1.

Direction of motion stereotypes

In general, users will expect the following movements to result in switching something on, or increasing the magnitude or intensity of something:

—turning a rotary control clockwise (except in taps and valves);

—moving a linear control downwards or towards the operator in Britain and Europe; but upwards and away from the operator in the USA;

—moving a linear control to the right (in both Europe and USA). In general, users will expect the moving parts of machinery or the indicators of displays to move in the same direction as the controls which operate them. Situations in which this expectancy may conflict with those given above should be avoided.

Feedback

The user should never be in any doubt as to whether or not he has operated or engaged a particular control. Toggle switches, levers, 'latching' push buttons, sliders and well designed rotary controls have built-in feedback. Return-action buttons should be designed to have a positive 'feel' as the button engages and (preferably) to make an audible click. Devices which lack these advantageous characteristics will require enhanced feedback in the form of an associated indicator light, etc. (Bleeping noises are infuriating to most people over the age of about 20.)

Design of common control devices

Most ergonomics reference works include specifications for the dimensions, etc. of particular controls. Each set of figures is a little different; those in table 26.1 are based on MIL-STD-1472C.

Table 26.1 Specifications for common control devices

Dimensions in mm, resistances in newtons (N), unless otherwise specified
Separations and resistances assume random (i.e. non-sequential) operation using one hand (or finger)
Separations are from edge to edge unless otherwise stated

a) Push buttons

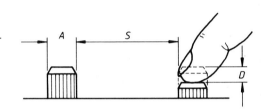

	Dimension A (diameter, or edge if square)		Displacement D		Resistance		Separation S	
Fingertip	min	max	min	max	min	max	min	pref
operated	10	25	2.8	11.0	2	6	13	50
Thumb or								
palm operated	19	—	2.8	23.0	3	38	25	150

For single finger sequential operation or for operation by several fingers minimum separation is 6 mm (25 mm preferred)

b) Toggle switch

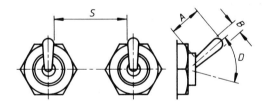

Dimension A		Dimension B		Resistance		Displacement D (2 position)		Separation S	
min	max	min	max	min	max	min	max	min	pref
13	50	3	25	2.8	4.5	30°	60°	19	50

For three setting positions (the maximum acceptable number) the minimum displacement between positions is 17° (25° preferred; 30° maximum)
For single finger sequential operation minimum separation is 13 mm (preferred 25 mm)
For simultaneous operation by several fingers minimum separation is 16 mm (preferred 19 mm)

c) Rocker switch

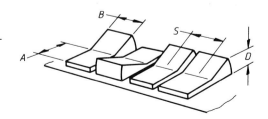

Dimension A		Dimension B		Displacement D		Resistance		Separation S	
min	max	min	max	min	max	min	max	min	pref
6	—	13	—	3	—	2.8	11	19	—

Table 26.1 (continued)

d) Rotary selector switch

Dimension A		Dimension B		Dimension C		Displacement D		Resistance		Separation S	
min	max	min	max	min	max	min	max	min	max	min	pref
25	100	–	25	16	75	15°	40°	115 mN.m	680 mN.m	25	50

For simultaneous operation with both hands minimum separation is 75 mm (125 preferred)

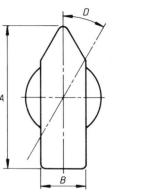
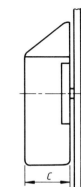

e) Knob (fingertip operation)

Dimension A		Dimension B		Resistance		Separation S	
min	max	min	max	min	max	min	pref
10	100	13	25	–	32 mN.m	25	50

For knobs greater than 25 mm diameter maximum resistance is 42 mN.m.
For simultaneous operation with both hands minimum separation is 50 mm (125 preferred)

f) Thumbwheel (continuous adjustment)

Dimension A		Dimension B		Resistance		Separation S	
min	max	min	max	min	max	min	pref
25	100	3	23	–	3.3	25	50

The standard quotes different figures for discrete thumbwheels

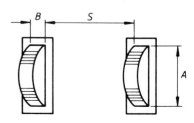

Table 26.1 (continued)

g) **Lever** (hand grasped)

Dimension A		Resistance			
		Forward		Sideways	
min	max	min	max	min	max
38	75	9	135	9	90

Displacement				Separation	
Forward D_1		Sideways D_2		S	
max		max		min	pref
360		970		50	100

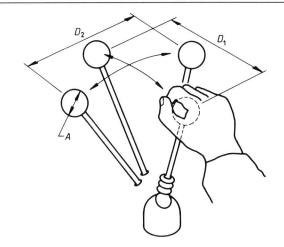

h) **Pedal**

	Dimension A		Dimension B		Displacement D		Resistance		Separation S	
	min	max	min	max	min	max	min	max	min	pref
Ankle movement	25	—	75	—	25	65	45	45	100	150
Leg movement	25	—	75	—	25	180	45	90	100	150

If the operator's foot is not to rest on the pedal minimum resistance is 18 N, otherwise 45 N as stated.
An alternative maximum resistance of 800 N is given for leg movement operation. Comparison with other sources suggests this would only be acceptable under exceptional circumstances.

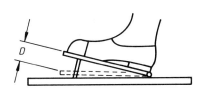

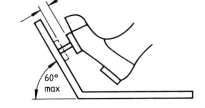

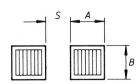

From MIL STD 1472C

Table 26.2 Specification for cranks

Dimensions in mm, resistances in newtons (N), unless otherwise specified
Separations and resistances assume random (i.e. non-sequential) operation using one hand (or finger)
Separations are from edge to edge unless otherwise stated
Minimum separation S is 75 mm.

Load	Handle						Turning radius					
	Length L			Diameter D			Rate below 100 r/min			Rate above 100 r/min		
	Min.	Pref.	Max.	Min.	Pref.	Max.	Min.	Pref.	Max.	Min.	Pref.	Max.
Light (less than 22 N — wrist and finger operation)	25	38	75	10	13	16	38	75	125	13	65	115
Heavy (more than 22 N — whole arm operation)	75	95	—	25	25	38	190	—	510	125	—	230

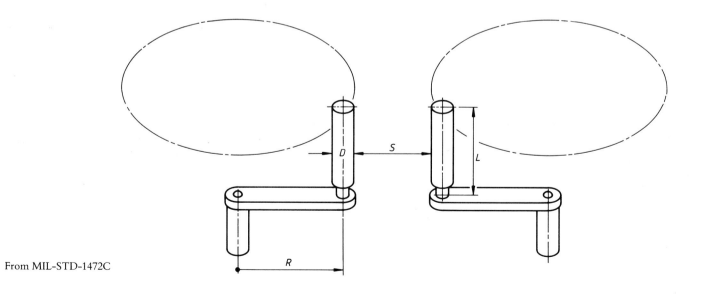

From MIL-STD-1472C

26.2 Vehicle controls

Tractor controls

ISO Technical Report TR 3778 deals with the *maximum* actuating forces required to operate the controls of agricultural tractors; its recommendations are given in table 26.3. The report acknowledges that *'these forces are not the optimum ergonomically'*.

Comment—It is important to emphasize that these are intended as maximum forces and that lower values would certainly be preferable. A brake pedal force of 600 N is likely to be beyond the reasonable capacity of some members of the user population (Pheasant and Harris 1982).

Table 26.3 Maximum actuating forces required to operate controls

Device to be operated	Type of control	Maximum actuating force to operate control	Note	
		N		
Service brake	Pedal	600	Pressure	It should be possible to achieve effective braking performance with these forces applied
	Hand lever	400	Traction	
Parking brake	Pedal	600	Pressure	
	Hand lever	400	Traction	
Clutch	Pedal	350	Pressure	
Dual clutch		400		
Power take-off coupling	Pedal	300	Pressure	
	Hand lever	200	Traction	
Manual steering system	Steering wheel	250	Applies when changing from forward drive into the angle of turn needed to achieve a turning circle of 12 m radius	
Power-assisted steering system with failure of the power-assisted steering force		600		
Hydraulic power lift system	Hand lever	70	Pressure and traction	

From ISO/TR 3778

Location of automobile controls

ISO 4040 deals with the location of hand-operated controls in passenger cars. There is of course a general requirement that such controls should be within the reach envelope as defined in ISO 3958 and given in section 5. However, it is also desirable that a reasonable degree of uniformity should exist between other vehicles in order to minimize the chances of operating the wrong control in an emergency. Three control zones are defined with respect to the axis and rim of the steering wheel as shown in figure 26.1. The parts of a control which are in contact with the hand are considered to sweep out an 'operational area' as they are moved between their various positions.

It is recommended that:

- The operating area of the headlights beam switching, optical warning and direction indicator controls shall be in zone 1. (The optical warning and headlights beam switching functions will be operated by the same control.)

- A portion of the operational area of the audible warning (horn) control shall be in either zone 1 or zone 2.

- The operational area of the master lighting control shall be to the left of the reference plane. (This is approximately the mid-line plane of the driver—its precise definition is complex.)

- The emergency braking control shall be to the left of the reference plane in right-hand drive cars and to the right of the reference plane in left-hand drive cars.

- The windscreen washer and wiper shall be operated by the same control which will generally be in zone 3.

- The master lights control shall *not* be operated by the same device as the audible warning, windscreen wiping, windscreen washing or direction indicators (unless it is operated using one of the modes to be avoided for the other control).

Table 26.4 and figure 26.2 give the preferred modes of operation for stalk controls mounted on or near the steering column.

ISO 3409 deals with the lateral spacing between and around the accelerator, brake and clutch pedals of cars. It specifies how such spacings should be measured but does not quote minimum, maximum or other recommended values. In the absence of such dimensional recommendations the standard seems rather pointless. Suitable figures are given in MIL-STD-1472C (see table 26.1).

Anthropometric and postural aspects of the design of the driver's workspace, with particular reference to the location of controls, are discussed in Pheasant (1986).

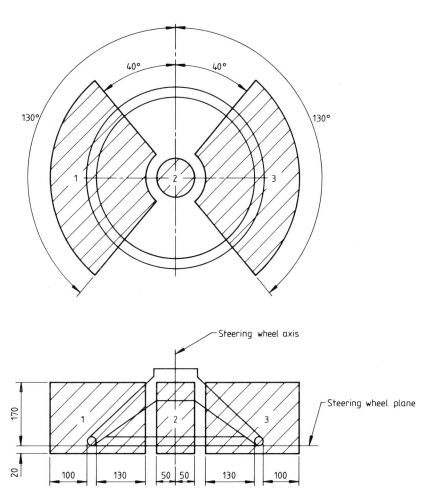

Figure 26.1 Control zones in cars with respect to axis and rim of steering wheel   From ISO 4040

Table 26.4 Requirements for modes of operation for stalk controls

When functions are operated by stalk controls mounted on or near the steering column (see figure 26.2), the preferred modes of operation and the modes to be avoided are as given in the following table.

Function	Preferred mode	Modes to be avoided	Secondary operational surfaces to be avoided
Master lighting switching	None	None	Secondary touch or proximity operational surfaces which are not protected from inadvertent operation (i.e. shielding, recessing, sequencing, etc.)
Headlights beam switching	Approximately parallel to the steering wheel axis	Directed towards the steering wheel axis Rotation approximately about the axis of the control	All
Audible warning	None	Approximately parallel to the steering wheel plane Rotation approximately about the axis of the control	All
Windscreen wiping	None	Approximately parallel to the steering wheel axis Directed towards the steering wheel axis NOTE — These do not preclude the automatic operation of wipers when washers are activated	Secondary touch or proximity operational surfaces which are not protected from inadvertent operation (i.e. shielding, recessing, sequencing, etc.) (for on–off only)
Windscreen washing	Directed towards the steering wheel axis or Approximately parallel to the steering wheel axis (to the right of the reference plane only)	None	All
Direction indication	Approximately parallel to the steering wheel plane	All others	All
Optical warning	Approximately parallel to the steering wheel axis	Directed towards the steering wheel axis Rotation approximately about the axis of the control	All

From ISO 4040

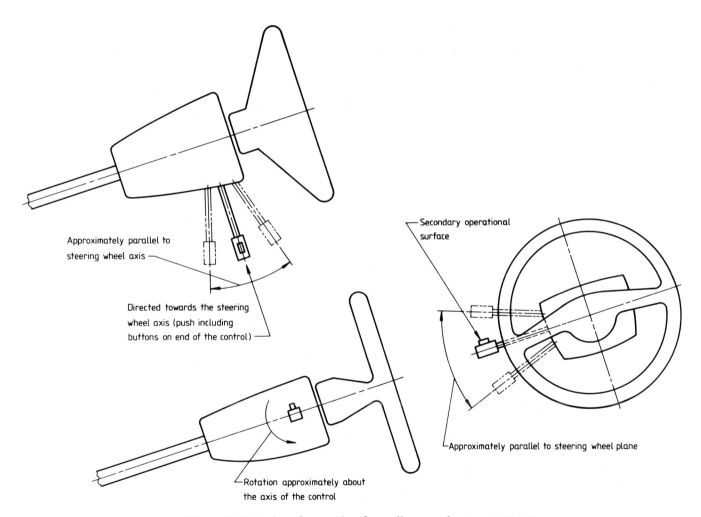

Approximately parallel to
steering wheel axis

Directed towards the steering
wheel axis (push including
buttons on end of the control)

Rotation approximately about
the axis of the control

Secondary operational
surface

Approximately parallel to steering wheel plane

Figure 26.2 Modes of operation for stalk controls   From ISO 4040

26.3 Keyboards

A number of standards deal with the design and layout of keyboards for typewriters (BS 2481, ISO 1090, ISO 1091) calculators and adding machines (BS 5478, ISO 1092, ISO 1093, ISO 3792) and office machines and data processing equipment in general (BS 4822, BS 5231, BS 5448, ISO 2126, ISO 3244, ISO 3791). There is considerable overlap between the recommendations of these standards and only a brief summary will be attempted here.

Alphanumeric keyboards

The basic 'QWERTYUIOP' arrangement of the alphanumeric keys on a typewriter (see figure 26.3) has not changed in almost a century and in spite of its manifest disadvantages (in terms of complexity and an inappropriate division of workload between the fingers, etc.) it is almost certainly with us to stay. The changes which have been suggested over the years, with the aim of rationalizing the arrangement, have not met with success: there is no reason to believe that similar attempts will be made any more successfully in the future.

Numeric keypads

The basic ten digit arrangement for the numerals on calculators, etc. is shown in figure 26.4, which is taken from ISO 3791.

The zero key (or keys if double or triple zeros are also required) should be located in the stippled area. The decimal point key should be located at the bottom right of the stippled area.

ISO 3791 states that 'to cover particular requirements' the keys in rows B and D may change places (ISO 1092 does not allow this for adding machines and calculators). The alternative arrangement, which is commonly encountered on telephones, has been shown to be ergonomically preferable (Conrad and Hull 1968).

Key spacing

ISO 1091 recommends a distance of 19 ± 1 mm between the centres of adjacent keys in a row and also between the centres of keys in adjacent rows. (The latter only applies to electric typewriters.) MIL-STD-1472C quotes a preferred size of 13 mm for the key itself with a spacing of 6.4 mm between keys.

Slope of keyboard

For calculators, etc. ISO 1092 recommends that the plane of the key top surfaces (P-P in figure 26.5) should make an angle α with the horizontal (H-H) of between 10° and 20°. This would be suitable for most other types of keyboard.

Displacement

BS 5478 states that the displacement required to operate a key should not exceed 7 mm.

Resistance

None of the British or International Standards quoted above gives a key resistance. MIL-STD-1472C gives the following:

	Numeric	Alphanumeric	Dual function
Minimum	1 N	250 mN	250 mN
Maximum	4 N	1.5 N	1.5 N

It is generally considered that, in order to give the operator adequate feedback, keys should have a 'positive snap action' and preferably make an audible click as well.

Additional information—A further discussion of the design of controls may be found in Grandjean (1981, Ch 9); Oborne (1981, Ch 6); Pheasant (1986, Ch 17).

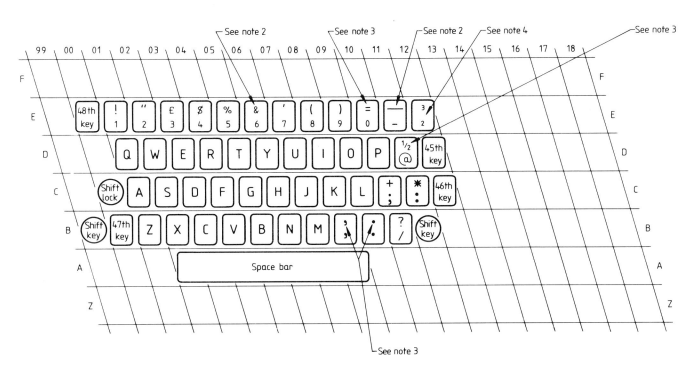

Figure 26.3 Typewriter keyboard layout   From BS 2481: Part 1

Notes
1. Information on the grid reference system used in this figure is contained in BS 5959.
2. The locations of 'ampersand' and 'underline' may be exchanged.
3. If this character is present on the keyboard, it shall occupy the position specified for it. If not present, it may be replaced by any character for for which a mandatory position has not been specified.
4. Recommended position for superscripts ^{2} and ^{3}.

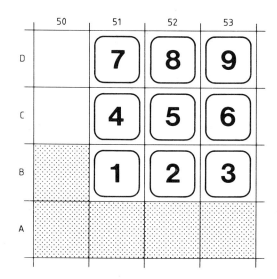

Figure 26.4 Keyboard layout for numerals
From BS 5478:Part 1

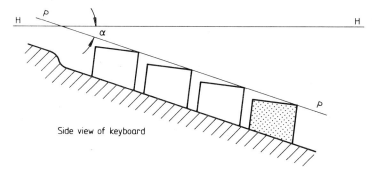

Figure 26.5 Slope of keyboard
From BS 5478: Part 1

Section 27 Human computer interaction

The interactions between human beings and computers constitute what is probably the most important area of progress in ergonomics at the present time. The ergonomic problems which computers pose may be analysed at three levels:

the hardware interface—that is, the physical characteristics of the computer equipment and the environment in which it is used (workstation design);

the software interface—that is, the process of communication between the user and the machine and the user's comprehension of this process (dialogue design);

the organizational interface—that is, the integration of one or more human beings and the machine(s) they use into a smoothly operating *socio-technical system*.

In the discussion which follows we shall only attempt to cover the first two.

27.1 The hardware interface—workstation design

The most important elements of a typical computer workstation have already been discussed elsewhere in this book.

- concerning keyboards see section 26.3
- concerning VDU screens see section 17.2
- concerning office furniture see section 22.2.

Ergonomically, there is no real reason to believe that VDU users require a different kind of furniture from other office workers. However, it is probably true that, given inadequate or unsatisfactory furniture, the problems suffered by VDU operators will be more severe—owing to the more stressful and posturally demanding nature of their task. The following points are commonly made:

- A raised reading stand is advantageous in order to bring 'copy' to the same level as the VDU screen.
- The screen should, if possible, be physically separate from the keyboard; so that the user can adjust its vertical and horizontal position to suit his own viewing requirements (see section 14). A design technique for determining the optimal height of a *fixed* VDU screen is given in PP 7310.
- The screen should have an adjustable tilting mechanism so that the individual user may angle it to suit his own line of sight and to avoid specular glare (see below and section 10.2).
- A relatively high-backed chair (backrest height approximately 500 mm) which would be beneficial for all office workers, is particularly advantageous for computer operators.

Lighting. High levels of illumination will make the VDU screen difficult to read—particularly if the screen has light characters on a dark background (negative polarity). Low levels make other office tasks difficult. The most commonly recommended compromise lighting level is 300 lx to 500 lx. For positive polarity screens (black characters on white) higher levels will be preferable.

Care should be taken to avoid glare—particularly *specular glare* caused by reflections of light fittings or windows on the VDU screen (see section 10.2).

- A typical terminal generates about the same amount of *heat* as an office worker—approximately 100 watts.

Some printers can produce as much as 70 dB to 80 dB of *noise*.

27.2 The software interface—dialogue design

The ergonomics of communication is discussed in section 18, much of which is relevant to the design of computer dialogues. The following specific points are compiled principally from Oborne (1985) and Ericsson (1983).

Command language

The greatest problem facing the novice computer user is generally the arbitrary and inconsistent nature of the instructions he is required to issue in order to store, retrieve or move items or files of information. (These instructions are sometimes known as the *command language*.) Syntax should, as far as possible, be consistent throughout a particular operating system—hence commas, spaces, etc. should always be used in the same way and in the same position within the 'sentences' of a command.

The *order of 'words'* within a sentence should, as far as possible, be similar to that of ordinary English. Hence, the command:

    INSERT, X, Y

should mean 'Insert item X into position Y' (which is compatible with English); rather than meaning 'Insert, into position X, item Y' (which is not compatible).

Similarly, the *meaning* of command words (such as LOAD, DELETE, DUMP, etc.) should, as far as possible, resemble the way in which they are ordinarily employed. For example, the term DUMP implies (to most people) the act of throwing something away—rather than putting it into a file.

Error messages should be as explicit as possible. In general, it makes sense to design such messages to be appropriate to the level of knowledge of a user who is likely to make such an error.

Instructions to the user should be made explicit. Hence, if the system requires a yes/no answer, the appropriate response should be indicated YES/NO, Y/N, etc.

Response time is the time that elapses between the last action of the user (keying in a message) and the appearance of the first displayed or printed character of the response. If this exceeds the time lag of normal conversation (two seconds to four seconds) people begin to suspect a breakdown of communication. Response times should therefore be both as short as possible (less than two seconds) and uniform in length. Where long delays are inevitable the system should (politely) inform the user.

Additional information—Extended treatments of human computer interaction include Cakir et al (1980), Ericsson (1983), Oborne (1985) and Grandjean (1986).

Section 28 Garment sizes

The sizing of clothes, particularly with respect to the design and distribution of a range of ready-to-wear items, is basically a problem in applied anthropometry. It is the example *par excellence* of fitting the product to the user. The commercial benefits to be gained from optimizing this match are considerable.

Size designation

With the exception of certain specialized items (listed below) only the *designation* of clothing sizes is standardized. This is the subject of a series of British Standards (BS 3666, BS 3728, BS 5511, BS 5592 and BS 6185) which are either identical to or else based upon items from a parallel series of International Standards (ISO 3635, ISO 3636, ISO 3637, ISO 3638, ISO 4415, ISO 4416, ISO 4417). The BS series will be discussed here.

The primary aim of this series of standards 'is the establishment of a size designation system that indicates (in a simple, direct and meaningful manner) the body size of the person that a garment is intended to fit . . . The size designation system is based on body and not garment measurements. Choice of garment measurements is normally left to the designer and the manufacturer, who are concerned with style, cut and other fashion elements, and who must make due allowance for garments worn beneath a specific garment'.

The *control dimensions* upon which the sizing system is based are defined in ISO 3635. These are: head girth, neck girth, chest girth (in men), bust girth (in women), underbust girth (measured just below the breasts in women), waist girth, hip girth, height (stature; or recumbent body length in infants not yet able to stand), outside leg length and inside leg length.

BS 3666 (women's wear), BS 6185 (men's wear), BS 3728 (children's and infants' wear) and BS 5592 (headwear) each specify the particular combination of controlling dimensions which shall be used to designate the size of a particular type of garment.

These measurements quoted in centimetres should appear on the garment's label—where practicable in the form of a pictogram (standardized in BS 5511). Additional garment measurements, considered to be of relevance, may be indicated separately. Examples (from BS 3666) are given in figure 28.1.

In the case of women's wear (BS 3666) an additional size code is also specified (table 28.1) and examples of how the size code number might be included on the label are given (figure 28.2).

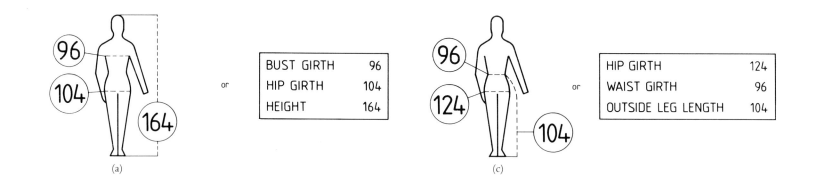

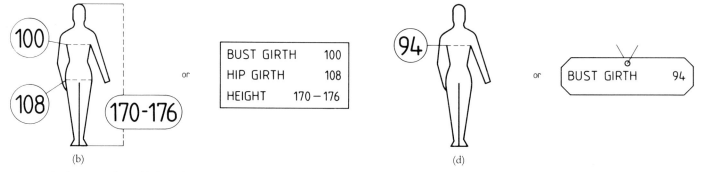

Figure 28.1 Examples of labels for women's outerwear   From BS 3666

or

HIP GIRTH	124
WAIST GIRTH	96
SKIRT LENGTH	66

Figure 28.1 (concluded)

Table 28.1 Size codes and associated body measurements

Dimensions in cm

Size codes	Body measurements			
	Hips		Bust	
	from	to	from	to
8	83	87	78	82
10	87	91	82	86
12	91	95	86	90
14	95	99	90	94
16	100	104	95	99
18	105	109	100	104
20	110	114	105	109
22	115	119	110	114
24	120	124	115	119
26	125	129	120	124
28	130	134	125	129
30	135	139	130	134
32	140	144	135	139

From BS 3666

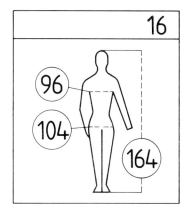
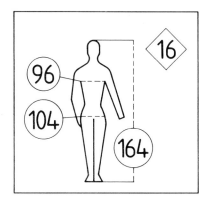

SIZE	16
BUST GIRTH	96
HIP GIRTH	104
HEIGHT	164

Figure 28.2 Examples of inclusion of size code number into label
From BS 3666

Specialized garments

Standards dealing with specialized garment types include:

BS 3783   X-ray lead-rubber protective aprons for personal use

BS 4171   Donkey jackets

BS 4676   Gaiters and footwear for protection against burns and impact risks in foundries

BS 4981   System of shoe sizing and marking (Mondopoint)

BS 6183   Protective equipment for cricketers

BS 6308   Men's uniforms

BS 6408   Clothing made from coated fabrics for protection against wet weather

Discussion—Essentially the task which faces the manufacturer or retailer of a range of ready-to-wear garments is:

1   to achieve an acceptable match with the maximum possible number of prospective purchasers;
2   to mimimize the number of sizes in any particular range.

These two objectives must, to some extent, be traded off against each other—in order to maximize the overall profitability of the range.

Major retailers, such as multiple chain stores, are naturally reticent about the details of their marketing strategies. But it would probably be true to say that decisions concerning the range of sizes of a particular garment to stock under particular circumstances, are largely made by trial and error: they are rarely (if ever) the product of any kind of rigorous scientific or statistical analysis. In general, the retailer will simply stock up on those sizes which have sold well in the past—and if a certain size consistently gets left on the shelf he will stock it in smaller numbers (or perhaps cease to stock it at all).

The disadvantage of the trial and error approach is that it provides the retailer with no information concerning those potential customers who fail to find a garment which fits them and do not purchase anything at all; these 'unsatisfied potential customers' might constitute 5% of the overall population or 50%—the retailer has no real way of knowing. In the absence of such information he cannot make an informed decision as to whether an increase or change in his range of sizes would be commercially beneficial.

A possible alternative approach could be devised, based upon anthropometric data of the kind given in table 3.1. There are two major obstacles to this approach:

1   The data which exist (at least in the public domain) may not be adequate for the purpose. In the case of British adults, there is an up-to-date and reasonably representative data set for men (WIRA, 1980); but the best available data for women are those of Kemsley (1957) which were collected in 1951 (and may not have been particularly representative of the general population even then). The relevant data given in table 3.1 are partly an updating of Kemsley's figures—based on an informed estimate of the ways in which the sizes and shapes of women have changed in the intervening decades—and partly estimates based on overseas data. It may well be that better data exist outside the public domain—it would be reasonable for a manufacturer or retailer to consider such data to be subject to commercial security. Extensive investigation has not revealed (to the author) the existence of 'private datasets' of any consequence, concerning British adults.

2 The statistical problems of optimizing a range of sizes, taking into account the various inter-correlated bodily dimensions involved in the design of a garment, are by no means simple.

Anecdotal evidence suggests that the problems which potential customers experience, in finding ready-to-wear garments that fit adequately, fall broadly into three categories:

1 The potential customer is 'outsized' with respect to the range of fittings commonly available. Suppose a retail outlet decided to stock women's frocks ranging from size 10 to size 22 (this is quite common). By definition these would fit busts from 820 mm to 1140 mm and hips from 870 mm to 1190 mm (BS 3666) which covers the 5th percentile to 95th percentile range of bust circumferences in table 3.1 and a somewhat greater range of hip circumferences. If the anthropometric data are correct (and as we have seen this is quite a big 'if') we should expect the 5 per cent of women, whose busts are larger than the 95th percentile, to have difficulty in finding a frock which fits. (The problems are presumably less acute for those women less than the 5th percentile.) It may well be perfectly acceptable to the retailer if one woman in 20 who wishes to buy a certain frock is forced to go away empty handed—but it is very annoying for the frustrated would-be customer. (Hence the success of mail order catalogues and specialist shops catering for the larger woman.)

2 The customer is within the range of available sizes as designated on the garment's label—but finds that the garment does not fit in other respects. (This is a shape problem rather than one of overall size.) Men's shirts are a notorious example. Sizes are designated by neck circumference. Anthropometrically, this is very poorly correlated with a dimension such as upper limb length—hence, the number of men who find their shirt sleeves either too long or too short is scarcely surprising.

3 The customer finds that the size designated on the label is unhelpful, since it does not indicate how 'generous' a fit is intended. The current standards are deliberately non-specific in this respect—in order to allow for styles ranging from 'skin-tight' to 'baggy'.

Appendix A

ISO 6385 Ergonomic principles in the design of work systems

(References in margin indicate section in main text)

0 Introduction

Technological, economic, organizational and human factors affect the work behaviour and well-being of people as part of the work system. The design of the work systems shall satisfy human requirements by applying ergonomic knowledge in the light of practical experience.

1 Scope

This International Standard establishes ergonomic principles as basic guidelines for the design of work systems.

2 Field of application

The ergonomic guiding principles specified in this International Standard apply to the design of optimal working conditions with regard to human well-being, safety and health, taking into account technological and economic efficiency.

NOTES

1 This International Standard shall be used in conjunction with other pertinent standards, regulations or agreements.

S21 2 Adaptation of this International Standard may be necessary in order to meet additional requirements of some categories of individuals, for example, in view of age or handicap, or in the case of exceptional working situations, or emergencies.

3 While the principles in this International Standard are oriented to industry, they are applicable to any field of human activity.

3 Definitions

3.1 work system: The work system comprises a combination of people and work equipment, acting together in the work process, to perform the work task, at the work space, in the work environment, under the conditions imposed by the work task.

3.2 work task: An intended outcome of the work system.

3.3 work equipment: Tools, machines, vehicles, devices, furniture, installations and other components used in the work system.

3.4 work process: The sequence in time and space of the interaction of people, work equipment, materials, energy and information within a work system.

3.5 work space: A volume allocated to one or more persons in the work system to complete the work task.

3.6 work environment: Physical, chemical, biological, social and cultural factors surrounding a person in his/her work space. However, social and cultural factors are not covered by this International Standard.

3.7 work stress (or external load): The sum of those external conditions and demands in the work system which act to disturb a person's physiological and/or psychological state.

3.8 work strain (or internal reaction): The effect of the work stress upon a person in relation to his/her individual characteristics and abilities.

3.9 work fatigue: The local or general non-pathological manifestation of work strain, completely reversible with rest.

4 General guiding principles

4.1 Design of work space and of work equipment

4.1.1 Design in relation to body dimensions

S2;S3 The design of the work space and work equipment shall take into account constraints imposed by body dimensions, with due regard to the work process.

The work space shall be adapted to the operator. In particular:

S6.1;
S23

a)   The working height shall be adapted to the body dimensions of the operator and to the kind of work performed. Seat, work surface, and/or desk should be designed as a unit to achieve the preferred body posture,

S6.1;
S22.1

namely trunk erect, body weight appropriately supported, elbows at the side of the body, and forearms approximately horizontal.

S22.1

b)   The seating arrangements shall be adjusted to the anatomic and physiological features of the individual.

S3;
S22

c)   Sufficient space shall be provided for body movements, in particular of the head, arms, hands, legs and feet.

S5

d)   Controls shall be within functional reach.

S4.1;
S4.2;
S7.3;
S7.4;

e)   Grips and handles shall suit the functional anatomy of the hand.

4.1.2   Design in relation to body posture, muscular strength, and body movements

The design of the work shall be such as to avoid unnecessary or excessive strain in muscles, joints, ligaments, and in the respiratory and circulatory systems. Strength requirements shall be within physiologically desirable limits. Body movements should follow natural rhythms. Body posture, strength exertion and body movement should be in harmony

S6;S7 with each other.

S6   **4.1.2.1** Body posture

Attention shall be paid primarily to the following:

a)   The operator should be able to alternate between sitting and standing. If one of these postures must be chosen, sitting is normally preferable to standing; standing may be necessitated by the work process.

S7.5;
S7.6

b)   If high muscle strength must be exerted, the chain of force or torque vectors through the body should be kept short and simple by allowing suitable body posture and providing appropriate body support.

S7.2

c)   Body postures should not cause work fatigue from prolonged static muscular tension. Alternations in body postures shall be possible.

S7   **4.1.2.2** Muscular strength

Attention shall be paid primarily to the following:

S7.1

a)   Strength demands shall be compatible with the physical capacities of the operator.

b)   Muscle groups involved must be strong enough to meet the strength demands. If strength demands are excessive, auxiliary sources of energy shall be introduced into the work system.

S6

c)   Maintenance of prolonged static tension in the same muscle shall be avoided.

4.1.2.3. Body movement

Attention shall be paid primarily to the following:

    a)   A good balance shall be established among body movements; motion shall be preferred to prolonged immobility.

    b)   Amplitude, strength, speed and pace of movements shall be mutually adjustable.

    c)   Movements with great accuracy requirements shall not entail exertion of considerable muscular strength.

    d)   Execution and sequencing of movements shall be facilitated by guiding devices, as appropriate.

4.1.3 Design concerning signals, displays, and controls

Pt. 3 **4.1.3.1** Signals and displays

S14 Signals and displays shall be selected, designed and laid out in a manner compatible with the characteristics of human perception.

In particular:

S17   a)   The nature and number of signals and displays shall be compatible with the characteristics of the information.

    b)   In order to achieve clear identification of information where displays are numerous, they shall be laid out in space in such a way as to furnish reliable orientation clearly and rapidly. Their arrangement may be a function either of the technical process or of the importance and frequency of use of particular items of information. This

S17.5
S26.1 may be done by grouping in accordance with the functions of the process, the type of measurements, etc.

S17   c)   The nature and design of signals and displays shall

ensure unambiguous perception. This applies especially to danger signals. Account shall be taken, for instance, of the intensity, shape, size, contrast, prominence, and the signal-to-noise ratio.

S26.1   d)   Rate and direction of change of display of information shall be compatible with rate and direction of change of the primary source of that information.

    e)   In protracted activities in which observation and monitoring predominate, overload and underload effects shall be avoided by design and layout of signals and displays.

S26 **4.1.3.2.** Controls

Controls shall be selected, designed and laid out in such a way as to be compatible with the characteristics (particularly of movement) of that part of the body by which they are operated. Skill, accuracy, speed and strength requirements shall be taken into account.

In particular:

S26.1   a)   Type, design and layout of controls shall correspond to the control task, taking into account human characteristics, including learned and innate responses.

S26.1   b)   Travel of controls and control resistance shall be selected on the basis of the control task and of biomechanical and anthropometric data.

S26.1   c)   Control movement, equipment response, and display information shall be mutually compatible.

S17
S26.1   d)   Function of the controls shall be easily identifiable to avoid confusion.

S17.5   e)   Where controls are numerous they shall be laid out so as to ensure safe, unambiguous and quick operation. This may be done similarly as for signals by grouping them according to their functions in the process, to the order in which they are used, etc.

f)   Critical controls shall be safeguarded against inadvertent operation.

Pt. 2   **4.2 Design of the work environment**

The work environment shall be designed and maintained so that physical, chemical and biological conditions have no noxious effect on people but serve to ensure their health, as well as their capacity and readiness to work. Account shall be taken of objectively measurable phenomena and of subjective assessments.

Depending on the work system it is necessary to pay attention in particular to the following points:

S4.3;   a)   The dimensions of the work premises (general layout,
S20   space for work, and space for work related traffic) shall
S21   be adequate.
S23

S8.6   b)   Air renewal shall be adjusted with regard to the following factors, for example:

— number of persons in the room;

— intensity of the physical work involved;

— dimensions of the premises (taking account of work equipment);

— emission of pollutants in the room;

— appliances consuming oxygen;

— thermal conditions.

S8   c)   Thermal conditions at the work place shall be

adjusted in accordance with local climatic conditions, taking into account mainly:

— air temperature;

— air humidity;

— air velocity;

— thermal radiation;

— intensity of the physical work involved;

— properties of clothing, work equipment, and special protective equipment.

S10.2   d)   Lighting shall be such as to provide optimal visual perception for the required activities. Special attention shall be paid to the following factors:

— luminance;

— colour;

— distribution of light;

— absence of glare and undesirable reflections;

— contrast in luminance and colour;

— age of operators.

S11   e)   In the selection of the colours for the room and for the work equipment, their effects on the distribution of luminances, on the structure and quality of the field of vision, and on the perception of safety colours, shall be taken into account.

S13   f)   The acoustic work environment shall be such that noxious or annoying affects of noise are avoided, including those effects due to outside sources. Account shall be taken in particular of the following factors:

S13.2
- sound pressure level;
- frequency spectrum;
- distribution over time;

S13.4
- perception of acoustic signals;

S13.3
- speech intelligibility.

S12   g)   Vibrations and impacts transmitted to man shall not attain levels causing physical damage, physio-pathological reactions or sensorimotor disturbances.

h)   Exposure of workers to dangerous materials and harmful radiations shall be avoided.

S8.2;   j)   During outdoor work, adequate protection shall be
S8.3   provided against adverse climatic effects (for example against heat, cold, wind, rain, snow, ice).

4.3 Design of the work process

The design of the work process shall safeguard the workers' health and safety, promote their well-being, and facilitate task performance, in particular by avoiding overloading and underloading. Overloading and underloading will result from transgressing, respectively, the upper or lower limits of the operational range of physiological and/or psychological functions, for example:

- physical or sensory overloading produces fatigue;
- conversely, underloading or work sensed as monotonous diminishes vigilance.

The physical and psychological stresses exerted depend not only on factors considered in 4.1 and 4.2 but also on the content and repetitiveness of operations and on the workers' control over the work process.

Attention shall be directed to implementation of one or more of the following methods of improving the quality of the work process:

a)   Having one operator perform several successive operations belonging to the same work function, instead of several operators (job enlargement).

b)   Having one operator perform successive operations belonging to different work functions, instead of several operators. For example, assembly operations followed by quality checks performed by the operator who also removes defects (job enrichment).

c)   Change of activity as, for example, voluntary job rotation among workers on an assembly line or in a team working within an autonomous group.

d)   Breaks, organized or non-organized.

In implementing the above measures, particular attention should be paid to the following:

e)   Variations in vigilance and work capacity over day and night.

S2;S7.1   f)   Differences in work capacity among operators, and changes with age.

g)   Individual development.

Bibliography of British and International Standards

All the British and International standards cited below and those of foreign national standards bodies may be bought from BSI Sales Department, Linford Wood, Milton Keynes MK14 6LE.

International Standards are issued by the International Organization for Standardization (ISO) and the International Electrotechnical Commission (IEC), both in Geneva.

Where a British Standard is identical to an International Standard its title is given under the International Standard only. Cross-references between identical International and British Standards are shown by this symbol: ≡

In other cases details of the British Standard are given and its correspondence to the international publications is shown thus:

= technically equivalent standard in which the wording and presentation may differ
≠ related standard

ISO 216-1975	Writing paper and certain classes of printed matter—Trimmed sizes—A and B series
ISO/R 226-1961	Normal equal-loudness contours for pure tones and normal threshold of hearing under free-field listening conditions = BS 3383
ISO/R 369-1964	Symbols for indications appearing on machine tools
ISO 780-1985	Packaging—Pictorial marking for handling of goods
ISO 1006-1983	Building construction—Modular coordination—Basic module
ISO 1040-1983	Building construction—Modular coordination—Multimodules for horizontal coordinating dimensions
ISO 1090-1981	Office machines and data processing equipment—Function key symbols on typewriters ≡ BS 2481:Part 2
ISO 1091-1977	Typewriters—Layout of printing and function keys ≡ BS 2481:Part 3
ISO 1092-1974	Adding machines and calculating machines—Numeric section of ten-key keyboards ≡ BS 5478:Part 1
ISO 1093-1981	Adding machines and calculating machines—Keytop and printed or displayed symbols ≡ BS 5478:Part 3
ISO 1791-1983	Building construction—Modular coordination—Vocabulary (Bilingual edition)
ISO 1999-1975	Acoustics—Assessment of occupational noise exposure for hearing conservation purposes
ISO 2126-1975	Office machines—Basic arrangement for the alphanumeric section of keyboards operated with both hands
ISO 2575-1982	Road vehicles—Symbols for controls, indicators and tell-tales
ISO 2631/1-1985	Evaluation of human exposure to whole-body vibration—Part 1: General requirements
ISO 2631/3-1985	Evaluation of human exposure to whole-body vibration—Part 3: Evaluation of exposure to whole-body z-axis vertical vibration in the frequency range 0.1 to 0.63 Hz
ISO 2767-1981	Road vehicles—Motorcycles—Symbols for controls, indicators and tell-tales
ISO 2848-1984	Building construction—Modular coordination—Principles and rules
ISO 2860-1983	Earth-moving machinery—Minimum access dimensions ≡ BS 6112
ISO 3055-1985	Kitchen equipment—Coordinating sizes

ISO 3098/1-1974	Technical drawings—Lettering—Part 1: Currently used characters ≠ BS 308
ISO 3244-1984	Office machines and data processing equipment—Principles governing the positioning of control keys on keyboards
ISO/TR 3352-1974	Acoustics—Assessment of noise with respect to its effect on the intelligibility of speech
ISO 3409-1975	Passenger cars—Lateral spacing of foot controls
ISO 3461-1976	Graphic symbols—General principles for presentation
ISO 3635-1981	Size designation of clothes—Definitions and body measurement procedure ≠ BS 5511
ISO 3636-1977	Size designation of clothes—Men's and boys' outerwear garments ≠ BS 3728
ISO 3637-1977	Size designation of clothes—Women's and girls' outerwear garments = BS 3666, ≠ BS 3728
ISO 3638-1977	Size designation of clothes—Infants' garments ≠ BS 3728
ISO/TR 3778-1978	Agricultural tractors—Maximum actuating forces required to operate controls
ISO 3791-1976	Office machines and data processing equipment—Keyboard layouts for numeric applications ≡ BS 5448
ISO 3792-1976	Adding machines—layout of function keyboard ≡ BS 5478:Part 2
ISO 3958-1977	Road vehicles—Passenger cars—Driver hand control reach
ISO 4040-1983	Road vehicles—Passenger cars—Location of hand controls, indicators and tell-tales ≡ BS AU 199
ISO 4129-1978	Road vehicles—Mopeds—Symbols for controls, indicators and tell-tales
ISO 4415-1981	Size designation of clothes—Men's and boys' underwear, nightwear and shirts ≠ BS 3728
ISO 4416-1981	Size designation of clothes—Women's and girls' underwear, nightwear, foundation garments and shirts = BS 3666, ≠ BS 3728
ISO 4417-1977	Size designation of clothes—Headwear ≡ BS 5592:1978
ISO 4869-1981	Acoustics—Measurement of sound-attenuation of hearing protectors—Subjective method ≡ BS 5108
ISO 5731-1978	Kitchen equipment—Limit of size
ISO 5732-1978	Kitchen equipment—Sizes of openings for built-in appliances
ISO 5970-1979	Furniture—Chairs and tables for educational institutions—Functional sizes ≠ BS 5873:Part 1
ISO 5982-1981	Vibration and shock—Mechanical driving point impedance of the human body
ISO 6385-1981	Ergonomic principles of the design of work systems
ISO 6512-1982	Building construction—Modular coordination—Storey heights and room heights
ISO 6513-1982	Building construction—Modular coordination—Series of preferred multimodular sizes for horizontal dimensions

ISO 6514-1982	Building construction—Modular coordination—Submodular increments
ISO 6549-1980	Road vehicles—Procedure for H-point determination
ISO 6727-1981	Road vehicles—Motorcycles—Symbols for controls, indicators and tell-tales
ISO 7000-1984	Graphical symbols for use on equipment—Index and synopsis
ISO 7001-1980	Public information symbols ≡ BS 6034
ISO/TR 7239-1984	Development and principles for application of public information symbols
ISO 7243-1982	Hot environments—Estimation of the heat stress on working man, based on the WBGT-index (wet bulb globe temperature)
ISO 7726-1985	Thermal environments—Instruments and methods for measuring physical quantities
ISO 7730-1984	Moderate thermal environments—Determination of the PMV and PPD indices and specification of the conditions for thermal comfort
IEC 73 (1984)	Colours of indicator lights and push buttons
IEC 417 (1973)	Graphical symbols for use on equipment With supplements (A, B, C, etc.)
IEC 425 (1973)	Guide for the choice of colours to be used for the marking of capacitors and resistors ≡ BS 5890
IEC 479-1 (1984)	Effects of current passing through the human body Part 1: General aspects
IEC 651 (1979)	Sound level meters

BS 381C:1980	Colours for identification, coding and special purposes
BS 1195	Kitchen fitments and equipment Part 1:1973 Imperial units with metric equivalents Part 2:1972 Metric units
BS 1244	Metal sinks for domestic purposes Part 1:1976 Imperial units with metric equivalents Part 2:1982 Stainless steel sink tops (excluding inset sinks)
BS 1319:1976	Medical gas cylinders, valves and yoke connections = ISO/R 32; ISO 407
BS 1413:1970	Page sizes for books
BS 1710:1984	Identification of pipelines and services ≠ ISO 508
BS 1753:1977	Safety requirements for children's cots
BS 1877	Part 10: 1982 Mattresses for children's cots, perambulators and similar domestic articles
BS 2481	Typewriters Part 1:1982 Keyboard arrangements ≠ ISO 2126, 2530 Part 2:1982 ≡ ISO 1090 Part 3:1982 ≡ ISO 1091
BS 2560:1978	Exit signs (internally illuminated)
BS 2747:1986	Code of practice for textile care labelling
BS 2770	≡ ISO 780
BS 3042:1971	Standard test fingers and probes for checking protection against electrical, mechanical and thermal hazard

BS 3044:1958	Anatomical, physiological and anthropometric principles in the design of office chairs and tables. By W F Floyd BSc PhD FInstP AMIEE and D F Roberts MA DPhil
BS 3121:1959	Performance requirements of fabrics described as of low flammability
BS 3254:1960	Seat belt assemblies for motor vehicles
BS 3383:1961	Normal equal-loudness contours for pure tones and normal threshold of hearing under free-field listening conditions = ISO/R 226
BS 3443:1968	Code of safety requirements for children's toys and playthings
BS 3456	Safety of household and similar electrical appliances Various parts
BS 3539:1962	Sound level meters for the measurement of noise emitted by motor vehicles
BS 3641	Symbols for machine tools Part 1:1971 General symbols ≠ ISO/R 369
BS 3666:1982	Size designation of women's wear = ISO 3637, 4416
BS 3693:1986	Recommendations for the design of scales and indexes on analogue indicating instruments
BS 3693A:1964	Recommended form of digits for use on dials and scales
BS 3693B:1964	Geometric construction of the recommended form of digits for use on dials and scales
BS 3705:1972	Recommendations for provision of space for domestic kitchen equipment
BS 3728:1982	Size designation of children's and infants' wear ≠ ISO 3636, 3637, 3638, 4415, 4416

BS 3783:1964	X-ray lead-rubber protective aprons for personal use
BS 3785:1964	Webbing safety harness for baby carriages and chairs and walking reins
BS 3881:1965	Safety requirements for carry cots
BS 4000:1983	Sizes of paper and board = ISO 216, 478, 479, 593
BS 4086:1966	Recommendations for maximum surface temperatures of heated domestic equipment
BS 4099	Colours of indicator lights, push buttons, annunciators and digital readouts Part 1:1986 ≡ IEC 73 Part 2:1977 Flashing lights, annunciators and digital readouts
BS 4125:1981	Safety requirements for child safety barriers for domestic use
BS 4139:1986	Safety requirements for perambulators (baby carriages)
BS 4142:1967	Method of rating industrial noise affecting mixed residential and industrial areas ≠ ISO/R 1996
BS 4171:1981	Donkey jackets
BS 4648:1970	Safety requirements for baby walking frames
BS 4676:1983	Gaiters and footwear for protection against burns and impact risks in foundries
BS 4787	Internal and external wood doorsets, door leaves and frames Part 1:1980 Dimensional requirements
BS 4792:1984	Safety requirements for pushchairs
BS 4800:1981	Paint colours for building purposes

BS 4822:1980	Keyboard arrangements of the graphic characters of the United Kingdom 7-bit data code, for data processing ≠ ISO 2530
BS 4863:1973	Safety requirements for rigid sided playpens for domestic use
BS 4875	Strength and stability of furniture Part 1:1985 Methods for determination of strength of chairs and stools Part 2:1985 Methods for determination of stability of chairs and stools Part 3:1985 Methods for determination of strength of settees Part 4:1985 Methods for determination of stability of settees Part 5:1985 Methods for determination of strength of tables and trolleys Part 6:1985 Methods for determination of stability of tables and trolleys Part 7:1985 Methods for determination of strength of storage furniture Part 8:1985 Methods for determination of stability of storage furniture
BS 4981:1984	Mondopoint footwear sizing and marking system ≠ ISO 2816, ISO 3355, ISO/TR 3836, ISO 3844
BS 5108:1983	≡ ISO 4869
BS 5231:1975	≡ ISO 3244
BS 5239:1986	Babies' dummies
BS 5252:1976	Framework for colour coordination for building purposes
BS 5304:1975	Code of practice for safeguarding of machinery
BS 5330:1976	Method of test for estimating the risk of hearing handicap due to noise exposure ≠ ISO 1999

BS 5378	Safety signs and colours Part 1:1980 Colour and design ≠ ISO 3864 Part 2:1980 Colorimetric and photometric properties of materials ≠ ISO 3864
BS 5395	Stairs, ladders and walkways Part 1:1977 Code of practice for design of straight stairs
BS 5423:1980	Portable fire extinguishers
BS 5448:1977	≡ ISO 3791
BS 5459	Performance requirements and tests for office furniture Part 1:1977 Desks and tables Part 2:1977 Adjustable chairs Part 3:1983 Storage furniture
BS 5478	Part 1:1977 ≡ ISO 1092 Part 2:1977 ≡ ISO 3792 Part 3:1982 ≡ ISO 1093
BS 5499	Fire safety signs, notices and graphic symbols Part 1:1984 Fire safety signs Part 2:1986 Self-luminous fire safety signs
BS 5511:1977	Size designation of clothes—Definitions and body measurement procedure ≠ ISO 3635
BS 5592:1978	≡ ISO 4417
BS 5619:1978	Code of practice for design of housing for the convenience of disabled people
BS 5656:1983	Safety rules for the construction and installation of escalators and passenger conveyors ≡ European Standard EN 115

BS 5655   Part 1:1986 Safety rules for the construction and installation of electric lifts
Part 5:1981 Dimensions of standard electric lift arrangements
Part 7:1983 Manual control devices, indicators and additional fittings

BS 5665   Safety of toys
Part 1:1979 Mechanical and physical properties ≡ European Standard EN 71:Part 1
Part 2:1978 Flammability of toys ≡ European Standard EN 71:Part 2

BS 5696   Play equipment intended for permanent installation outdoors
Part 1:1986 Methods of test
Part 2:1986 Construction and performance
Part 3:1979 Code of practice for installation and maintenance

BS 5722:1984   Flammability performance of fabrics and fabric assemblies used in sleepwear and dressing gowns

BS 5799   Children's high chairs and multi-purpose chairs for domestic use
Part 1:1986 High chairs

BS 5810:1979   Code of practice for access for the disabled to buildings

BS 5815:1979   Cotton and man-made fibre blend sheeting, sheets, pillowslips, towels and napkins for use in the public sector

BS 5852   Fire tests for furniture
Part 1:1979 Methods of test for the ignitability by smokers' material of upholstered composites for seating
Part 2:1982 Methods of test for the ignitability of upholstered composites for seating by flaming sources

BS 5873   Educational furniture
Part 1:1980 Functional dimensions, identification and finish of chairs and tables for educational institutions ≠ ISO 5970
Part 2:1980 Strength and stability of chairs for educational institutions
Part 3:1985 Strength and stability of tables for educational institutions

BS 5890:1980   ≡ IEC 425

BS 5925:1980   Code of practice for design of buildings: ventilation principles and designing for natural ventilation

BS 5940   Office furniture
Part 1:1980 Design and dimensions of office workstations, desks, tables and chairs

BS 5969:1981   ≡ IEC 651

BS 6034:1981   ≡ ISO 7001

BS 6100   Glossary of building and civil engineering terms
Various parts

BS 6112:1983   ≡ ISO 2860

BS 6183   Protective equipment for cricketers
Part 1:1981 Batting gloves, leg guards and boxes

BS 6185:1982   Size designation of men's wear

BS 6217:1981   ≡ IEC 417A, 417B, 417C, 417D

BS 6222   Domestic kitchen equipment
Part 1:1982 Coordinating dimensions ≠ ISO 3055, 5731, 5732

BS 6308:1982   Men's uniforms

BS 6336:1982   Guide for the development and presentation of fire tests and for their use in hazard assessment

BS 6344   Industrial hearing protectors
Part 1:1983 Ear muffs

BS 6408:1983	Clothing made from coated fabrics for protection against wet weather
BS 6472:1984	Guide to evaluation of human exposure to vibration and shock in buildings (1 Hz to 80 Hz)
BS 6473:1984	Protective hats for horse and pony riders
BS 6539:1984	Fireguards for use with solid fuel appliances
BS 6595:1985	Safety requirements for baby nests
BS 6652:1985	Packagings resistant to opening by children
BS 6750:1986	Modular coordination in building
BS 8206	Lighting for buildings Part 1:1985 Code of practice for artificial lighting
BS AU 143c:1984	≡ ISO 2575
BS AU 185:1983	Seat belt booster cushions
BS AU 186:1983	Carry cot restraints
BS AU 199:1984	≡ ISO 4040
PD 6446:1970	Recommendations for the coordination of dimensions in building. Combinations of sizes
PD 6504:1983	Medical information on human reaction to skin contact with hot surfaces
DD 22:1972	Recommendations for the coordination of dimensions in building. Tolerances and fits for building. The calculation of work sizes and joint clearances for building components
DD 32:1974	Guide to the evaluation of human exposure to whole-body vibration = ISO 2631-1985
DD 43:1975	Guide to the evaluation of exposure of the human hand-arm system to vibration
PP 1550:1986	Playing safe with British Standards
PP 7307:1986	Graphical symbols for use in schools and colleges
PP 7308:1986	Engineering drawing practice for schools and colleges
PP 7310:1984	Anthropometrics: an introduction for schools and colleges by S T Pheasant

Other References

Bennett C. 1977. *Spaces for People—Human Factors in Design*. Englewood Cliffs: Prentice Hall

Boyce P R. 1981. *Human Factors in Lighting*. London: Applied Science Publishers

Burns W. 1973. *Noise and Man*. London: John Murray

Cakir A; Hart D J and Stewart T F M. 1980. *Visual Display Terminals*. Chichester: John Wiley

CIBS. 1984. *Code for Interior Lighting*. The Chartered Institution of Building Services, London

Clark T S and Corlett E N. 1984. *The Ergonomics of Workspaces and Machines—A Design Manual*. London: Taylor and Francis

Conrad R and Hull A J. 1968. The preferred layout for numeral data entry keysets *Ergonomics*. **11**, 165-174

Damon A; Stoudt H W and McFarland R A. 1966. *The Human Body in Equipment Design*. Cambridge, Mass: Harvard University Press

Davis P R and Stubbs D A. 1977, 1978. Safe levels of manual forces for young males *Applied Ergonomics,* **8**, 141-150; 219-228 *Applied Ergonomics*, **9**, 33-37

DEF-STAN-00-25 Part 3, Issue 1. 1984. *Human Factors for Designers of Equipment Part 3: Body Strength and Stamina*. Ministry of Defence

DIN 31 001, Part 1. 1983. *Safety Distances for Adults and Children*. Berlin: Deutsches Institut für Normung e.V

DIN 66 234. *VDU Work Stations*
Part 1. 1980. *Geometric design of characters*
Part 2. 1983. *Perceptibility of characters on screens*
Part 3. 1981. *Grouping and formatting of data*
Part 5. 1981. *Coding of information*
Part 6. 1984. *Workstation design*

Part 7. 1984. *Design of the workspace by ergonomics; lighting and arrangement.* Berlin: Deutsches Institut für Normung e.V

Easterby R and Zwaga H (eds). 1984. *Information Design—The Design and Evaluation of Signs and Printed Material.* Chichester: John Wiley

Ericsson. 1983. *Ergonomic Principles in Office Automation.* Bromma: Ericsson Information Systems AB

Fanger P O. 1973. *Thermal Comfort.* New York: McGraw Hill

Fowler H W. 1983. *A Dictionary of Modern English Usage,* 2nd edition, edited by Gowers, Sir E. Oxford University Press

Goldsmith S. 1976. *Designing for the Disabled,* 3rd edition. London: RIBA

Grandjean E. 1981. *Fitting the Task to the Man: An Ergonomic Approach,* 2nd edition. London: Taylor and Francis

Grandjean E. 1986. *Ergonomics in Computerized Offices.* London: Taylor and Francis

Hartley J. 1978. *Designing Instructional Text.* London: Kogan Page

Hopkinson R G and Collins J B. 1970. *The Ergonomics of Lighting.* London: McDonald

HSE. 1976. *Lighting in Offices, Shops and Railway Premises:* Health and Safety at Work Booklet No 39A. London: HMSO.

HSE. 1978. *Code of Practice for Reducing the Exposure of Employed Persons to Noise.* Health and Safety Executive, London: HMSO

HSE. 1983. *Visual Display Units.* Health and Safety Executive, London: HMSO

Inman V T; Ralston H J and Todd F. 1981. *Human Walking.* Baltimore: Williams and Wilkins

Kemsley W F F. 1957. *Women's Measurements and Sizes.* Cheltenham Press

Knight I. 1984. *The Heights and Weights of Adults in Great Britain.* London: HMSO

Kryter K D. 1970. *The Effects of Noise on Man.* New York: Academic Press

McCormick E J and Saunders M S. 1982. *Human Factors in Engineering and Design.* New York: McGraw Hill

MIL-STD-1472 C. 1974. *Human Engineering Design Criteria for Military Systems, Equipment and Facilities.* Washington DC: US Department of Defense

Murrel K F H. 1969. *Ergonomics—Man in His Working Environment.* London: Chapman and Hall

NIOSH. 1981. *Work Practices Guide for Manual Lifting.* National Institute for Occupational Safety and Health, Cincinnati, Ohio 45226

Noble J. 1982. *Activities and Spaces. Dimensional Data for Housing Design.* London: The Architectural Press

Oborne, D J. 1981. *Ergonomics at work.* Chichester: John Wiley

Oborne, D J. 1985. *Computers at work—A Behavioural Approach.* Chichester: John Wiley

Parker J F and West V R (eds). 1973. *Bioastronautics Data Book.* NASA SP-3006, National Aeronautics and Space Administration, Washington DC

Pheasant S T. 1983. Sex differences in strength—some observations on their variability. *Applied Ergonomics,* **14**, 205-211

Pheasant S T. 1986. *Bodyspace—Anthropometry, Ergonomics and Design.* London: Taylor and Francis

Pheasant S T and Harris C M T. 1982. Human strength in the operation of tractor pedals. *Ergonomics,* **25**, 53-63

Singleton W T (ed). 1982. *The Body at Work.* Cambridge University Press

Spencer H. 1969. *The Visible Word.* London: Lund Humphries

Thompson D and Booth R T. 1982. The collection and application of anthropometric data for domestic and industrial standards. *Anthropometry and Biomechanics: Theory and Applications,* eds. Easterby R; Kroemer K H C and Chaffin D B. New York: Plenum Press

Tinker M A. 1963. *Legibility of Print.* Ames: Iowa State University Press

Troup J D G and Edwards F C. 1985. *Manual Handling—A Review Paper.* London: HMSO

Tutt D and Adler D (eds). 1979. *New Metric Handbook.* London: Architectural Press van Cott H P and Kinkade R G (eds). 1972. *Human Engineering Guide to Equipment Design.* Washington DC: US Department of Defense

WIRA. 1980. *British Male Body Measurements.* WIRA Clothing Services, Leeds

Woodson W E. 1981. *Human Factors Design Handbook.* New York: McGraw Hill

Woodson W E and Conover D W. 1964. *Human Engineering Guide for Equipment Designers.* Berkeley: University of California Press

Wright P and Barnard P. 1975. 'Just fill in this form'—a review for designers *Applied Ergonomics,* **6**, 213-220

Index